D0776356

"How do you tell sor   ıe Bible what
it's about in a way 1   By the end of
this book Mark You   y but not before
retelling the biblical narrative in a remarkably straightforward yet
compelling form, with gripping illustrative stories of his own from
decades of ministry as an overseas missionary, seminary professor
and president, pastor, husband, father, grandfather, and friend to
many. A book you won't want to put down!"

Craig L. BLOMBERG

Distinguished professor of New Testament, Denver Seminary

"From introduction to endnotes, *One True Story, One True God* was for
me a breath of fresh air."

Mart DeHAAN

Senior advisor of ministry content, Our Daily Bread Ministries

"When it comes to the Bible, it's easy to miss the forest for the trees,
making it difficult even to articulate what the book is all about. But in
One True Story, One True God, Dr. Mark Young takes us above the tree
line so that—from the twin peaks of redemption and mission—we can
trace the spine of the all-embracing narrative. From the creation of
the cosmos to the making of all things new, Dr. Young artfully bridges
Scripture's individual events and critical characters to its grand
story—the story that causes us to change the way we see ourselves,
our world, and our God."

Joseph R. DODSON

Associate professor of New Testament, Denver Seminary

"I spent way too many years nervously wringing the hands of
my heart because a few, mostly well-intentioned, teachers had
wielded the Bible as a club and convinced me that God exhaled
with disappointment every time He glanced in my oh-so-imperfect
direction. When I finally began to get the message that *One True
Story, One True God* so beautifully expounds on—that our Creator
Redeemer's compassion is what drives the biblical narrative and
that Scripture is not punitive but instead proves He's been in the
process of redeeming us into a perfectly loving relationship with him
all along—it was like wading into a cool, clear stream after barely
surviving a long, hot journey through the desert."

Lisa HARPER

Author and Bible teacher

"In our ever-changing world where many are searching for answers, our ability (or inability) to describe the Bible as the incredible story of redemption can make a big difference in winning souls to Christ. *One True Story, One True God* by Dr. Mark Young provides a wonderful context for seeing how our individual stories fit into God's overarching love story. Everyone has a story and God's desire is for all to ultimately come to know Him. This book is both needed and relevant for all believers at such a time as this. I highly recommend it."

John K. JENKINS Sr.
Senior pastor, First Baptist Church of Glenarden, MD

"Brilliantly insightful and beautifully inspiring—this is a compelling invitation to live into the grand story of God's redemptive mission in the world."

Philip MILLER
Senior pastor, The Moody Church, Chicago, IL

"If you've ever been intimidated, confused, dumbfounded, or intrigued by the Bible, open this book and start reading! Mark Young is an honest soul who asks the questions we all ask about the Bible. But also, he's a guide, capable of walking us through those questions to the practical and promise-filled answers he's discovered himself—answers that changed his life and can change ours as well."

Elisa MORGAN
Speaker, author, and cohost of Discover the Word *and* God Hears Her

"There's much insight and wonder to underline, savor, delight in, and enjoy in Mark Young's rich and wonderful exploration of the incomparable story of God's mission to rescue and redeem his people—the chronicle called the Bible. A deft explorer, knowing teacher, and kind leader, Young guides even novice Bible readers on a smart, sharp, clear journey to answer the question: what's this book about? Indeed, who is this book about and who is it for? Young answers good, deep, and well."

Patricia RAYBON
Author, My First White Friend, I Told the Mountain to Move, *and* One Year God's Great Blessings Devotional

ONE TRUE STORY, ONE TRUE GOD

ONE TRUE STORY

WHAT THE BIBLE IS ALL ABOUT

ONE TRUE GOD

MARK S. YOUNG

Our Daily Bread
Publishing™

Library of Congress Cataloging-in-Publication Data

Names: Young, Mark, 1956- author.
Title: One true story, one true God : what the Bible is all about / Mark Young.
Description: Grand Rapids : Our Daily Bread Publishing, [2021] | Includes
    bibliographical references. | Summary: "Gain a new understanding of
    God's redemptive plan through the story of the Bible and find out your
    purpose in accomplishing that plan"—Provided by publisher.
Identifiers: LCCN 2020041718 | ISBN 9781640700000 (paperback)
Subjects: LCSH: Bible—Introductions.
Classification: LCC BS475.3 .Y69 2021 | DDC 220.6/1—dc23
LC record available at https://lccn.loc.gov/2020041718

Printed in the United States of America
21 22 23 24 25 26 27 28 / 8 7 6 5 4 3 2 1

For Priscilla,

life partner in the big story

CONTENTS

ACKNOWLEDGMENTS

How do you turn four decades of teaching notes, lectures, sermons, articles, and conversations into a book? Turns out you can't. You have to write a book. And that takes far more help from caring and talented people than I ever imagined.

Debra Anderson and John Sloan helped me find my voice and make it something folks might want to read. The generosity of Ben and Heather Crane and Don and Patty Wolf nurtured my soul. The Board of Trustees at Denver Seminary gifted me with blocks of time to write. Kristen Beall checked the biblical references and endnotes for accuracy. Ty Heckelmann kept the office and my life in order. Writing a book and running a school are less compatible than I thought they would be. Ty somehow made it all work.

For months my dad, Gene Young, has been asking me when "the book" was going to be finished. Since he's within sight of his ninetieth birthday, his eagerness to read it added a measure of urgency to the writing process!

No one has shaped my life and, therefore, this book more than Priscilla. She lives into the big story of the Bible consistently and passionately. Her encouragement sustained me through the writing process. She would not let me give up when writing was the last thing I wanted to do. Her wisdom and her love for Jesus are found on every page.

Mark Young

THE QUESTION THAT CHANGED THE WAY I READ THE BIBLE

I ran down a broad hallway at Charles de Gaulle Airport in Paris, looking frantically for the departure gate for my flight. I was alone, a non–French speaker, and late for my flight.

I passed bakeries, espresso bars, and cafés that I would have loved to enjoy. But my incoming flight had arrived late and my connection was extremely tight. To make matters worse, my coach ticket, a last-minute purchase, had no assigned seat number. "You can get it at the gate," the travel agent had told me.

I had seen my flight number and gate on the departures board. I knew where I was supposed to go but I didn't know how to get there. A good guess finally found me sprinting down the right concourse. But when I got to the gate, there was no one around. "They must have closed the doors," I moaned, "and I've missed my flight."

Just then a gate attendant appeared out of the jetway and asked, "Are you Mr. Young?"

"Yes," I panted.

"Mr. Young, we do not have a seat for you," the woman said.

Oh, no. Visions of time lost, negotiations for new flight connections, and missed appointments back in Dallas began to flash through my mind. This is not the phone call I wanted to make to my family tonight. She must have seen the disappointment on my face.

"No, Mr. Young, we don't have a seat for you in coach, but we do have a seat for you in our business class." And she handed me a boarding pass.

A seat in business class? Is that really what she said? I had never sat in business class before, but the seats sure looked a lot roomier than the shoeboxes we were crammed into in coach. I could spread out and do some work. Or sleep. I headed down the jetway before she could change her mind!

Indeed, the seats in business class were bigger, comfier, and spread farther apart. Just what I needed after a long and stressful week.

I thought about what I could do to make sure I wouldn't be bothered during the long flight ahead. I had it. I'd lay open on my lap the one book that most people don't want to talk about with a stranger: the Bible. That ought to give me peace without interruption for the eight-hour flight. And that's just what I did.

As the plane gained altitude after takeoff, however, the young businessman, sitting in the seat next to mine, pointed at my Bible, and said in French-accented English, "And what is that book about?"

I was stunned and I was stumped. Two degrees from two theological seminaries, and I couldn't answer his question. I knew the parts of the Bible, original languages of the Bible, theology explaining the Bible, but I couldn't give a simple answer to his question. I'd taught in seminaries and spent time on the mission field. And I didn't have a response for this young man.

I fumbled through an answer, saying something like the book was about God and his Son, Jesus Christ, and forgiveness and grace and salvation. He smiled and sat back in his seat, nodding politely but giving the distinct impression that there'd be nothing in that book for him. That it wasn't something that could be read with interest.

The biggest jolt to my system did not come from my lackluster description of the book that was in my lap or of what had turned out to be a struggling explanation of the gospel (which was not even the question the young man had asked). The biggest jolt was that I truly couldn't explain in simple terms what the book I'd given my life to understanding was really about. I couldn't tell its story. I knew how to study the Bible, but I did not know how to *read* it. I could take it apart to analyze it in its most detailed minutiae, but I couldn't put the pieces back together. Kind of like Humpty Dumpty.

I continued to dwell on our discussion long after the flight had ended. Why couldn't I answer his question? Why couldn't I state what the Bible is about? The Bible has shaped my thinking and my life for decades. Perhaps it means so much to me that I hesitated to give a quick answer because I was afraid it wouldn't come close to demonstrating the Bible's great value. Maybe I marvel at the complexity and beauty of the Bible so much that I couldn't come up with an answer that would do justice to just how wonderful it is.

That question—"What's that book about?"—started me on a journey of discovery. And that journey led me to see that the Bible is a story masterfully crafted through the telling of many shorter stories. That question and that journey ultimately led to this book, my invitation for you to join me on the journey of learning to read the Bible as a story so that we can answer the question, "What's that book about?"

PART ONE

STORY

Everybody loves a great story. It's in our DNA. Stories shape our thinking more than logical arguments and bulleted lists of facts. They touch our emotions and values in ways that data and information can't. Through stories we "connect the dots" of perceptions, data, findings, arguments, and experiences. As one scholar put it, "The human mind is a story processor, not a logic processor."[1]

We all live by some story and we use that story to answer life's most important questions. We tell it to ourselves all the time. "We are, as a species, addicted to story. Even when the body goes to sleep, the mind stays up all night, telling itself stories."[2]

We not only live by that story, we love by it. We might even be asked to die for it. That's why the question we need to ask, but often find too intimidating to seriously consider, is this: "Is the story I live by true?"

CHAPTER

1

THE ONE TRUE STORY

That flight didn't just take me from Paris to Dallas. It took me to a new way of thinking about the Bible. What we think about the Bible determines how we read it. No matter what level of training or experience we have in studying it, we all start with some assumptions about the nature of the Bible itself. I like to say it this way, "Everybody starts somewhere when they read the Bible." And "story" is a good place to start.

The World Is Full of Stories

The world is full of stories. Every culture has its own collection. Some stories create our identities and shape our deepest values. Often, these stories are expressed in religious traditions. Most religions, whether formal or folk, create some sense of past, present, and future through stories that are told generation after generation. These stories shape the way we think about the nature and identity of spiritual realities, the nature of humanity, and the interaction between the spiritual and physical realms. Interestingly, every worldview does practically the same thing. A worldview is the way we see life. It is built on assumptions about the nature of reality, the nature of humanity, and the relationship between the two. Those assumptions are often framed in stories. And as we learn and tell our interpretation of our own history, our own stories, we deepen our sense of identity.

British theologian Lesslie Newbigin, who lived as a missionary in South India for much of his adult life, notes, "All of human life is shaped by some story: 'The way we understand human life depends on what conception we have of the human story.'"[1] The Bible is that kind of life-shaping story. Newbigin goes on to say that the Bible, as universal history, tells the whole story of the world from beginning to end. And every other story is at best only a partial telling of the true story of the world.

What Newbigin means is that all other worldview-shaping stories have at best one piece or a corner or a part of the puzzle but not the whole. The Bible claims to be *the* one true story. That is an audacious claim. It claims to be the story that fills in the gaps in all other stories and provides correction to errors they may contain. The Bible claims to be the only story that tells the beginning-to-end story of the one true God.

Claiming to be the one true comprehensive story isn't just audacious; in a pluralistic world it is offensive. We know there are many competing stories by which people make sense of the world and find their sense of purpose. We might be tempted to think that the Bible is irrelevant in a world like ours, so completely out of step with modern sensibilities that it can't possibly be what it claims to be. But we have to remember that when the Bible was composed, both in the ancient Near East and in first-century Greco-Roman society, the world was already full of other stories.

Ancient Egypt's Pyramid Texts regarding the afterlife of the pharaoh predate the writings of Moses (Genesis–Deuteronomy) by a thousand years. The Babylonian *Epic of Gilgamesh* may well be the world's earliest written story. It narrates a hero's journey to find the secret to eternal life. Hinduism's holy, moral, and philosophical text, the *Rig-Veda*, was likely completed before the first Old Testament books. These writings are not all stories per se, but all purport to answer universal human questions about life, death, the nature of the gods, and mankind's responsibilities.

The authors of all the books of the Bible lived in contexts that were just as pluralistic as the world you and I live in now. Every nation, every people group, had their own gods and stories that narrated how human life was formed and how people ought to live. In the ancient world there were many different stories narrating how human history was unfolding and how the gods were engaged in it. It is in this kind of context that the Bible was written, and its authors never shy away from, never back down from, the claim that the Bible tells the one true story of the one true God and his involvement in human history.

The Bible is a big story built out of several smaller ones. And when we say the Bible is a big story, we're saying that it addresses the big questions that people live by yet may not explicitly talk about. The big questions of life require a big story to answer them.

Philosophy is a discipline that attempts to answer the big questions of life. But stories, analogies, histories, tales, and tragedies may actually help us think about the big questions of life more effectively than the complex arguments and obscure terminology that characterize many works of philosophy. It turns out that a good story—much more than nonfiction texts, tight logical arguments, or bulleted lists of ideas—not only captures our attention, it changes our beliefs. One researcher noted that "stories cultivate our mental and moral development" as they arouse curiosity and keep the reader emotionally engaged.[2] It is no accident that our omniscient God chose to reveal himself to us through a story. After all, no one understands humanity more than humanity's Creator.

What the Bible Isn't

No matter our education, profession, upbringing, or native language, we all use our own assumptions, experiences, culture, and traditions as lenses when we try to make sense out of what we read in the Bible. So, it's no wonder that there are several views of the nature of the Bible and approaches to interpreting it. Some of them are insightful and helpful, but most are pretty limited in scope. Some approaches lead to an accurate understanding of a text; others lead people astray. And sometimes the assumptions people have about the Bible lead to unrealistic expectations about what they will gain from reading it.

In order to read the Bible in a way that allows us to understand it, we need to clarify what we think it is. And in order to do that, it might be a good idea to carefully delineate what the Bible isn't.

I often hear people talk about the Bible as if it were a collection of ideas about God. Indeed, we come to know God through reading the Bible. In its pages, we see his character, intentions, and actions. For example, in the Bible we see that God is all-powerful, all-wise, loving, just, and faithful, to name just a few of his attributes. Often when I'm reading a passage, one of the first questions I ask is, "What can I learn about God in these verses?" The Bible does give us lots of information about who God is and what he's accomplishing in the world.

But the Bible is more than just a compilation of wonderful truths about God. And we run the risk of emphasizing some of those truths at the expense of others if we read the Bible only in this way. What the Bible tells us about God is framed by a big and powerful story that unfolds what we can know about him.

I also see people reading the Bible as a kind of handbook for happy living. In fact, I would say this is the most common way we read the Bible. We're all looking for help in figuring out how to live in a way that is pleasing to God. There's nothing wrong with that desire. We tend to see the Bible, therefore, as a collection of wise tips about life's most pressing challenges and responsibilities: how to be married, how to be single, how to raise kids, how to manage money, how to lead an organization. And those are just a few of the issues. The list seems almost endless.

Certainly, the Bible does give us some clear ideas about how to lead a life that is not only pleasing to God, but ultimately pleasing to ourselves and to others as well. It's good for us to read the Bible for guidance. This demonstrates our high regard for Scripture's truth and ability to shape our lives. But if we read it as primarily a handbook for happy living, we reduce the Bible to some kind of manual. That diminishes the scope and power of the story of the Bible and focuses our attention on just a few particular verses that meet our own personal needs. When we read it this way, we tend to take to heart only what encourages us and ignore the commands or examples that seem difficult or odd. This approach makes the Bible say less than it was written to say.

Sometimes I hear people talk about the Bible more like a textbook than a handbook. In this approach we can be tempted to make the Bible say more than it was written to say. For example, the Bible has been approached as a textbook for biology, economics, psychology, and other areas of disciplined inquiry and research.

Surely, the Bible contains accurate observations about creation, human behavior, and the nature of the relationship between the two. But it was not written as a textbook to logically and sequentially lay out all that can be known about these realities. The ability humans have to do scientifically rigorous research is a marvelous gift of God that creates tremendous benefit for us. And our knowledge of the world God created expands continually through such research. The Bible provides the framework within which our research must be interpreted, and it serves as a guide for us to use such research in the way we live our lives. However, if we read the Bible as a scientific textbook, we're trying to make it say more than it was written to say.

Other people see the Bible as an important collection of good, even great, works of literature. While this viewpoint rightly identifies and appreciates the Bible's many literary genres such as poetry, letters, law, prophecies, and historical narratives, it can often mask any sense of continuity or structure in the Bible. This approach highlights the beauty of the Bible's words but downplays the remarkable continuity we see in the accounts of the various authors of Scripture.

We certainly should read and interpret the various books of the Bible in light of their literary qualities—this is part of good interpretation. But viewing the Bible as just a great work of literature tends to overlook the startling truth that the Bible claims to be inspired by God, "God-breathed," to use Paul's language in 2 Timothy 3:16. It is the inspiration of the Holy Spirit that allows a multitude of authors who wrote over a period of some fourteen centuries to craft a cohesive narrative. No other book makes that claim.

Perhaps you've heard still other viewpoints like the Bible is a legislative standard of morality, a guide for personal decisions, or even a devious work meant to control people.[3] Or perhaps you've personally approached the Bible in other ways at various times in your life. Maybe you've closed your eyes, opened the Bible, and asked the Lord to guide your finger to a verse he wants you to meditate on that day. Some call that the "helicopter" approach to reading the Bible. Unfortunately, this approach can lead to inaccurate interpretation and inappropriate application of the verses your finger lands on. An oft-used example would be if your finger landed on Matthew 27:5, "Then he [Judas] went away and hanged himself." Not finding the encouragement you were seeking in that verse, you close your eyes and try again. This time your finger points to Luke 10:37, "Jesus told him, 'Go and do likewise.'" That's probably not the inspiration you were looking for to start your day.

So, if all of the above approaches have some serious deficiencies and help us realize what the Bible isn't, then what is the Bible? How should we approach it? It's pretty simple. We need to approach the Bible as a story with a beginning and an end, and a narrative arc that flows through all its pages. When we begin to view the Bible as a story, we find an amazing cohesiveness and an abiding clarity about the "big" questions that every person asks. We also find in the story the audacious claim about God that he desires to have a relationship with us. Because I had never learned to read the Bible as a story, I couldn't answer my seatmate on that flight out of Paris. Even more, I wasn't fully seeing or living into God's purpose for me.

The Universal Story

The Bible's beginning has an end in mind. The very first phrase in the Bible, "In the beginning God . . ." implies a set period of time. That means at the beginning of the story there is already a foreseen end.[4] And since God is the one who starts the story, he is the one who will bring it to completion. This story will begin and end somewhere, and everything in between is not just randomly thrown together. With God's intention to finish the story established at the very beginning, we're put on alert that this book is to be read as one cohesive story.

The Bible gives us the privilege of understanding who God is and gives us direction by which we should live. And it does so with truth and beauty. But the Bible does far more than that. It unfolds the one true story about the one true God's engagement in human history and human destiny. That's a story we must not ignore.

Because the Bible claims to tell the story of the one true God, we need to read it as the universal story. It's a transcendent story that answers the big questions of life. When I began to read it that way, it changed the way I think about God, what it means to be a human being, and how I am to live. It drove me to think again about the big questions. And because it answers those questions through the unfolding of its story, the answers were deeper and richer than any I'd found before.

Stories touch the deeper spaces of our hearts and help resolve questions we may not even know we've been asking. Stories allow us to observe someone else's life and struggles and then connect our own to theirs. Letting our walls down by emotionally connecting with the characters in a story opens us to learn more. "Studies show that when we read nonfiction, we read with our shields up. We are critical and skeptical. But when we are absorbed in a story, we drop our intellectual guard. We are moved emotionally, and this seems to make us rubbery and easy to shape."[5] This reaction puts us into a posture to ask the story our own questions regarding truth, reality, existence, and purpose.

That's why Jesus taught primarily through stories called parables. He explained this to his disciples in Matthew 13:11–13 (MSG): "You've been given insight into God's kingdom. You know how it works. Not everybody has this gift, this insight; it hasn't been given to them. Whenever someone has a ready heart for this, the insights and understandings flow freely. But if there is no readiness, any trace of receptivity soon disappears. That's why I tell stories: to create readiness, to nudge the people toward receptive insight. In their present state they can stare till doomsday and not see it, listen till they're blue in the face and not get it."

Lesslie Newbigin recalls the insightful observation of a friend and Hindu scholar of world religions who talks about the Bible as a unique history and story of the human race: "I can't understand why you missionaries present the Bible to us in India as a book of religion. It is not a book of religion—and anyway we have plenty of books of religion in India. We don't need any more! I find in your Bible a unique interpretation of universal history, the history of the whole of creation and the history of the human race. And therefore a unique interpretation of the human person as a responsible actor in history. That is unique. There is nothing else in the whole religious literature of the world to put alongside it."[6]

The Bible, the story about the God who engages humanity from the beginning to the end of time, is the kind of story that begs us to ask the big questions. It invites us to imagine the character of the one true God and to find ourselves in the story of his involvement with humanity as created, sinful, redeemed, restored, and purposeful creatures. No other story does that.

If we're going to attempt an answer to the question that the French businessman asked me on that airplane, we could say, "Well, it's a book about God." We could definitely start there, couldn't we? But the Bible is about more than that. As we read it, we begin to understand God's character *and* how he is present and involved in the world. I think it's fair to say if someone asked you, "What's that book about?" you could safely say it's about God's involvement in all of human history and, ultimately, in human destiny.

The Bible answers the deep question, "Is there a God?" with a resounding "Yes!" And it never backs down from that claim. But the Bible tells us much, much more about God. It reveals to us a God who desires to be known and worshiped. This desire of God is not driven by any need in him for attention or praise—because God lacks nothing. Rather, it is driven by his knowledge that if humans know him and worship him, they will find life and satisfaction in him that can be found nowhere else. In other words, God's involvement in human history from the beginning to the end of all things is driven by his perfect love. Because of his love, he wants us to experience life in its fullest, life lived with a joy and satisfaction that mirrors what he experiences in the Trinity. And he knows that this kind of life can be found only in relationship with him.

The Bible not only tells us what God is like, it tells us about ourselves—who we are, how we came to be who we are, and how we can live in relationship with God himself. The Bible actually talks more about humanity than it talks about God. Contrary to what some may think, the Bible is not just a story of religious ideas and laws; it's the story of human history. It introduces us to some of the most interesting characters we could ever imagine. Some of the people in the Bible make me cringe. Some of them make me laugh. Some of them inspire me, while others make me angry. The Bible is a very human story.

We ought not to think the Bible presents only perfect people with perfect lives. Nothing could be further from the truth. Within its pages we see God using those whom he directly speaks to and those who are deaf to his voice. We see him involved with those who worship him and those who curse him. And we even see him use those who don't know him—like a hard-hearted pharaoh in Egypt, a pagan king in Persia, and dismissive Roman rulers in Judea—to accomplish his purposes. The Bible makes it clear that God is guiding, directing, and overseeing a rebellious and weak humanity toward an end that he has ordained.

The Bible's scope, diversity, complexity, and power take my breath away. But that was part of the problem when I tried to come up with an answer to the question posed by that businessman on the plane. I hadn't ever tried to look beyond those traits and see the whole. Somehow, I had to step back from the individual events and characters that the Bible introduces us to and just think about the whole story from beginning to end. And as I do that, two words come to mind: *redemption* and *mission*.

2

ONE BIG STORY, TWO BIG WORDS

y wife and I moved to Colorado in 2009 after living in several other places in the United States and overseas. Living in Denver, we get to see the majestic Rockies towering over our city, holding court over the high plains of eastern Colorado. Those mountains have captured our hearts. All you have to do is look west and they'll be there. Always there, always beckoning.

A Magnificent View

The highest peaks in the Colorado Rockies are called "fourteeners" because they soar to an elevation more than fourteen thousand feet above sea level. Snow-covered much of the year, the peaks of these mountains sit at least two thousand feet above tree line. Soon after arriving in Colorado, we decided to hike to the summit of a fourteener. On the way to the top, we hiked through majestic pine forests and beautiful alpine tundra with its unique array of grasses, rocks, and spectacular wildflowers. Above tree line the true splendor of the Rockies stretched out before us.

Peak after snow-covered peak, sharp ridges, deep cirques with crystal blue alpine lakes and trees struggling to climb up the steep rock-strewn slopes all put on a show for us as we emerged into the high alpine terrain. Looking out from the summit of a fourteener, all the various parts of the landscape were put into perspective. We could see how the pine and aspen forests blanketed the lower elevations of the mountainsides, how they thinned out and eventually grew no higher up the slope. We saw alpine lakes turn into rivulets and eventually rivers.

None of this was visible while we were still below timberline where our line of sight was obstructed and perspective limited. Once we saw the whole, the parts made so much more sense. That doesn't mean the parts don't have their own beauty, but by themselves they can mask the scope and majesty of the whole.

If you think of the various plots, scenes, and characters of the Bible like the many different parts and views of a mountain landscape, a truth comes into view. We often only focus on individual characters, events, or verses in the Bible instead of the big story. When we do that, we are reading below tree line and the majesty of the whole story is blocked from our view. And if we focus only on one scene or passage without a sense of how it fits into the whole, it is like seeing only one part of the mountain landscape and missing the scope and grandeur of all that lies before us.

Multiple Plotlines

The Bible is a complex book. There's no doubt about that. But its complexity doesn't make it impossible to understand. Sure, there are multiple stories in the Bible and some of them seem disconnected from one another, but some of the best and most poignant stories utilize the storytelling tool known as parallel plotlines. Two of my favorites are the Oscar-winning movie *Crash* (2004) and the network TV series *This Is Us* (2016–). In *Crash*, director and screenwriter Paul Haggis weaves together the stories of several different people in the city of Los Angeles as their lives "crash" into each other. The multiple story lines keep me glued to the screen as I see glimpses of how all of these different characters and events are related around powerful themes of racism, alienation, common humanity, and hope.

This Is Us, on the other hand, follows the lives of triplets as they navigate the intricacies of tragic loss, disappointment, love, and family. Creator Dan Fogelman weaves past, present, and future events into an ever-evolving story line. There are enough glimpses into the future to keep me anticipating what's next and enough forays into the past to create powerful insights and reflection. As the characters' lives unwind and bump into each other along the way, we keep wondering if and how the story's going to reach a conclusion. We watch with the hope of resolution but remain unsure how it will all come together and make sense. That anticipation, the hope that at the end it will all make sense, keeps us watching. That's great storytelling.

There is no question that the Bible has multiple plotlines. It is a story built out of stories. And sometimes those stories seem to have little in common with one another. I used to wonder what on earth Job the sufferer, Judah the coconspirator, Joshua the mighty warrior, Jabez the land-grabber, Josiah the reformer king, Jeremiah the weeping prophet, and James and John the disciples called the sons of thunder all have to do with one another. How do their stories crash into each other and somehow create a sense of anticipation that it's all headed somewhere?

All of their stories find meaning in their relationship to God. Across many centuries and even millennia, these characters and their stories create a plotline that makes sense only if it is attached to the God of the Bible, the one who creates, directs, and completes his will through them for the sake of all of humanity. The earth and its people are his story.

Therefore, for us to find the overarching story of the Bible in the dozens of stories it contains, we have to see how God is at work writing the big story of his engagement in all human history. We need to get above the tree line. That's where we will find God to be bigger and more majestic than we've ever seen him before. When we step back from the details of the Bible and think about the whole story from beginning to end, what do we see of God and his engagement in human history? As noted before, two words come to the fore: *redemption* and *mission*. Together they capture the idea that everything God does carries out his plan to rescue his people and restore creation to all that he created it to be. Let's take a closer look at those two words.

REDEMPTION. We use the word *redemption* in different contexts to mean slightly different things. For example, when some people hear the word, they think about the act of redeeming air miles for free trips or redeeming points on a rewards credit card for cash. Exchanging air miles for free trips or points on a credit card for cash are both similar in this way: we assign value to something that has no real worth until exchanged. The miles and points just sit in an account until they are exchanged for airline tickets or cash.

Others might think about how *redemption* can mean "recapture," such as redeeming a day that has gone downhill. In this context, redemption means making something good out of something that went bad. It implies buying back something that we felt was lost.

But redemption can also be used in a much more powerful and meaningful way than we commonly use it. Before I tell you one of those hard-to-believe redemption stories, let's look at some results from a recent survey about passengers on airplanes: fifty passengers actually found a lasting love connection on an airplane, one in seven found a long-lasting friendship, and one in eight have established helpful business connections.[1] In fact, more than half of all passengers reported that they have had friendly conversations on their flight. Considering that more than four billion passengers booked flights in 2017,[2] that means there are a lot of friendly conversations, business deals, and romantic connections taking place on airplanes. And this provides the backdrop for a redemption story.

Temple Phipps knew what rejection felt like. She had been through a divorce earlier in life and now at forty-two, she still dreamed of becoming a mother. But the right husband hadn't shown up and the right details hadn't come together. She shared her dream with her supportive mother and friends and explored options for adoption and foster care. She was stable, successful, and hopeful, but she was turned down by the adoption agencies because she couldn't provide a two-parent household.[3]

When Temple planned a trip home to Raleigh, North Carolina, from Atlanta, Georgia, she was able to get a seat on an earlier flight than the one she had booked.[4] A twenty-four-year-old passenger who was eight months pregnant filled the empty seat next to her. Samantha Snipes was obviously discouraged and nervous. She, too, wasn't supposed to be on that particular flight, but had missed her connection in Atlanta.

Temple put Samantha at ease in the first few minutes they sat together. Temple learned that Samantha was at a pivot point in her life. Her baby boy had been fathered by an abusive man, and she had been taking refuge in the home of her alcoholic mother. Bedridden from depression in recent months,[5] she was now flying to meet a boyfriend she'd met online several weeks ago.

Samantha talked about how she had considered putting her

baby up for adoption, but her mother had said she wanted to keep the child. Samantha knew her mother's home wasn't a healthy environment, but she felt caught. She wasn't thinking clearly. She was flying out to meet a new boyfriend, and she wasn't at all clear about what she was going to do when the baby arrived in another month. She tearfully shared with Temple during their hour-long flight that she had no real support and was scared to live on her own.[6]

In that brief window of time, the two women established a strong connection and didn't stop talking for the entire duration of the flight. Then Temple revealed her longtime desire to have children. She talked about her supportive family and friends.[7] She gave Samantha her phone number and told her she'd love to adopt Samantha's son. Three days later, Samantha called Temple. The five-pound baby boy had been born early, and she wanted Temple to come see him, to be with him, and even to consider being his mother.

It took Temple just twenty minutes to drive to the hospital. When Samantha watched her hold and nurture baby Vaughn in her arms for an hour, Samantha knew Temple would love him in ways she didn't know how to. Temple officially adopted Vaughn, and her act of love rescued both that baby boy and his birth mother from a broken future.

But that's not the end of the story. Temple helped Samantha get back on her feet. Samantha moved to North Carolina, started a photography business, now talks regularly to Temple, and is a part of the family. She sees Vaughn often, including on his birthday. Temple made a way for Samantha to step out from under shame and live with freedom. Samantha says, "To me she is a mother, a sister, and a great friend . . . she's given me more of a family than I ever had."[8] What a powerful story of redemption.

Temple, Samantha, and Vaughn's story shows us the sheer

power of redemption, how it can change the entire landscape of someone's life from abandoned to embraced, from endangered to empowered, and from injured to healed. Rescue and restore. Those are the two key actions in redemption. That's what we see in the story of the Bible. God enters human history with a clear purpose, a mission to rescue humanity from its plight and restore it to the way he created people to live.

Powerful and dramatic, like an epic motion picture, such is the story of the Bible. It's a simple story but its plot unfolds through a complex and diverse set of short stories, teaching, and poetry. The plot unfolds like this. God creates all things, including humans, to enjoy life in its fullest. But the first humans rebel and bring upon themselves the penalty of death. God intervenes to rescue humanity from experiencing the full consequences of their rebellion and to restore them to what he planned for them. It's a redemption story like no other, the foundation for countless other redemption stories penned through the centuries. God's great act of redemption is ultimately accomplished by the death of Christ on the cross, and it will be completed when he returns to fully restore the heavens and the earth to the fullness of life that God created them to enjoy. That's the story of the Bible. It's the story of God's redemptive mission. That's what the Bible is about. That's the answer I should have given the man on the flight from Paris to Dallas.

When we think about redemption, it's easy to slip into thinking we can do something to redeem ourselves, that we're the main actor in the plan of redemption. That's the way we most often use the word today. For example, sometimes in sports a star player does something reckless or careless that causes her team's chances for victory to be put in jeopardy. But later in the game she pulls off an incredible athletic feat that leads the team to victory. After seeing her make the play that saved the game, we'd probably say something like, "It's a good thing she made that play. She redeemed herself with that one." Notice the phrase "she redeemed herself." We like to think that we can make up for our past mistakes, clean up our messes, and make things right, the way they ought to be. Although that may be true in some circumstances, when it comes to our relationship with God, nothing could be further from the truth.

Believing we can in some way pay God back for our own sins strips us of the privilege of seeing and experiencing God's power to redeem us. It is in our helplessness to make things right that God steps into our lives, rescues us from the destructive power of our sin, and gives us the life and relationship with him we thought we could never possibly have. Redemption is God's work. And it's his mission. He desires that all people know and worship him. And he will do whatever is necessary to make that possible for everyone.

MISSION. Everybody starts somewhere when they think about God. All of us ground our understanding of God in who we think he is and how his character is to be understood. Some start to look at his character through the lens of his sovereignty. Others begin with his love. Some see everything through the lens of his power and presence, while still others focus upon his mysterious ways.

All of these aspects of his character appear in Scripture. But which of these attributes ought to be the lens through which we see God? That's the question different theologies and traditions have fussed over for centuries. Each elevates one of God's attributes above the others and then sees everything else we can know about God through that lens. And then we select certain verses from the Bible to justify our choice. But, if we can step back from the particular passages we choose to justify our approach and think about the whole story of the Bible, another way to frame what we think about God comes clearly into sight—the *mission of God.*

If you've been around churches or Christians much you've probably heard the word *missions* used a lot. Generally speaking, *missions* refers to the activities of a select group of people who leave the comforts of their homeland and go somewhere to tell people about Jesus. But note that in this book we're using the singular form of the word: *mission.* And we're also not using the term to describe something that we do. We're using the word to describe something that God does.

The *mission of God* is the best phrase to describe how we see God engaging humanity when we consider the whole big story of the Bible. First, God always takes the *initiative* in his relationship to humanity. His is the first action in the Bible (creation), and his is the last (the making of a new heaven and a new earth). Everything God does flows out of his desire to be known and worshiped by all. He takes the initiative to make himself known.

Second, God always acts *intentionally,* with purpose. Nothing God does is random. His every act is purposeful, designed and executed to accomplish his purpose. *Mission* can be defined as sustained effort to accomplish a goal. When we think of God taking the initiative and intentionally doing what is necessary to accomplish his purpose, that leads us to mission. God is guiding all of creation and human history to the end that he has foreseen and ordained when all of the earth knows him, worships him alone, and finds the fullness of life in him.

Third, God's desire to be known springs from his eternal *love.* He reveals himself to all because he knows that only in knowing and worshiping him can the fullness of life be found. When God takes the initiative to accomplish his purpose, he *moves toward* humans. This "movement" of God is best illustrated in the nature of the relationship between the three persons of the

Trinity—Father, Son, and Holy Spirit. The Father sends the Son and the Father and the Son send the Holy Spirit. The *sending of God* is a phrase that beautifully expresses the triune personhood and movement of the God of the Bible. God is always moving toward us.

But how does all of this add up to mission? Think about it this way. "Mission" implies taking charge and setting direction. It describes actions that lead to the accomplishment of one's purpose. Because of God's desire to be known and worshiped so all people can find true life in him, he does whatever is necessary to accomplish that desire.[9] My wife, Priscilla, and I described it this way in a chapter we coauthored, "The Bible narrates the story of how God makes his desire a reality. God's eternal desire becomes God's mission. From Genesis to Revelation the Bible describes how God acts in human history so that all may know and worship him."[10]

Christopher J. H. Wright makes the claim that "mission is what the Bible is all about."[11] That's a bold claim, one that some might dispute. Isn't it an overstatement to say that the Bible is all about any single thing? Indeed, the Bible speaks to many different issues of life and reveals many different aspects of God's character. But when we step back from the details and ask, "What's the big story of the Bible about?" God's redemptive mission leaps from its pages. As Wright says, "The whole Bible renders to us the story of God's mission through God's people in their engagement with God's world for the sake of the whole of God's creation."[12] The Bible is the story of God's mission.

The mission of God is a powerful theme that answers one of the most difficult questions we face in reading the whole Bible as one big story—the seemingly irreconcilable differences between the Old and New Testaments. Some see the two Testaments as disconnected books that present two very different pictures of God. But the mission of God provides a powerful unifying theme between the two Testaments. God's desire to be known and worshiped by all "gives structure to the whole Bible."[13] The mission of God "unifies both Old and New Testaments and coordinates the various themes into a single motif."[14] The mission of God is the same in the Old Testament and in the New: God does whatever is necessary so that all peoples can worship him and find life in him.

Redemption is God's answer to the three problems that humanity can never solve on its own—sin, death, and evil. God steps into our dilemma and does what we could never do ourselves—set us free from the bondage of sin, death, and evil and restore us to life in relationship with him. That is redemption and redemption is God's mission. That's why we can assert that the Bible is the story of God's redemptive mission. And that's what I wish I had said to the man who asked me, "What's that book about?"

One Beautiful Tapestry

The Bible is one big story summarized in two big words—*redemption* and *mission*. We will have much more to say about these two big words in the rest of this book. For now, let's focus on another characteristic of this saga of redemption and mission. It unfolds through five key elements. They are essentially chronological in that they move the story forward from beginning to end, but each element also appears repeatedly throughout. Think of them as five different colored threads that are woven into a tapestry that tells a story.

The five threads that are woven together into the big story of the Bible are (1) creation, (2) fall, (3) redemption, (4) consummation, and (5) the people of God's mission.

Here's the challenge as we look at these five threads in the chapters that follow. Like being below the tree line, we don't want to lose sight of the whole story as we look at the details of each thread. Just as there is a spectacular view of God's creation tapestry from the high peaks of the Rockies, we can enjoy a spectacular view of God's redemptive mission as we keep our eyes on the big story of the Bible.

PART TWO

PLOT

Nobody likes wandering around lost. We all need to believe we're getting somewhere when we're on a journey. The same thing is true when we're reading a story.

Without a plot there is essentially no story. Through its plot a great story takes the reader on a journey. The plot is the spine of a story, connecting its settings, characters, and events. It's also the energy of a story, moving the reader toward the conclusion the author has foreordained. A good plot keeps us reading, anticipating what comes next, reacting to unexpected developments, and believing that it's all going to be worth it in the end.

It's tempting to think of the Bible as just a collection of unrelated stories. But that would be a mistake. The Bible is far more than that. It's a sprawling epic whose plot spans human history, gathering up and connecting hundreds of settings, characters, and events into one grand story.

We must never lose sight of that story as we read the Bible.

3

CREATION

The Bible begins with a bang! Its first words are a bold, un-equivocal, in-your-face assertion that God is the Creator of everything. "In the beginning God created the heavens and the earth." Genesis 1:1 goes off like an alarm. It warns us that we're about to read a story unlike any other story about a God unlike any other god.

And it never backs down from that claim.

Sometimes I wish the Bible gave us a chance to warm up to the idea that God created all things rather than slapping us in the face with that fact right off the bat. I started reading the Bible seriously in the 1970s when I was a college student. We worried a lot about defending the trustworthiness of the Bible, especially the opening chapters of the Bible. I remember people saying, "If you can't trust everything in the Bible, you can't trust anything in the Bible." So, we spent a lot of time trying to read Genesis 1 and 2 like a science textbook. Unfortunately, in our efforts to prove that these chapters were scientifically true, I'm afraid we lost sight of the grandeur of the story they introduce and the magnificence of the God they reveal.

Don't get me wrong. It's important to believe the Bible doesn't contain any errors in all that it affirms. I believe that. But we have to admit that a lot of Bible readers have struggled to reconcile what the Bible says with what we have learned, and continue to learn, about creation through science. Unfortunately, some people try to make us think that the Bible and science are at war with one another. That's a lie. Christians don't have to choose between the Bible and science. Through the years biblical scholars, theologians, and scientists have come up with several credible approaches to integrating scientific knowledge with a responsible interpretation of the opening chapters of Genesis.[1] No matter what approach we take on this question, however, we dare not lose sight of the fact that these opening chapters introduce a magnificent story that demands to be taken seriously.

The creation account in Genesis chapters 1 and 2 may not have been written necessarily to tell us *how long ago* the world came into existence, but it was definitely written to demonstrate *who* created the world, *what kind* of world God created, and *why* God created it. In essence, we can summarize this triad with the following: God made it all, it was all good, and he did it so that we can know him. These chapters set the tone for the rest of the Bible. They let us know that we cannot know God truly apart from knowing him as creator God. In fact, the rest of the story makes no sense if God isn't the Creator of everything.

God as Creator

God's identity as Creator is reaffirmed consistently throughout the Bible. For example, Psalm 146:6 declares, "He [the LORD] is the Maker of heaven and earth, the sea, and everything in them—he remains faithful forever." The Bible just assumes that God is the Creator of all; it never tries to prove that point.

The Bible frequently reminds us that, as Creator, God is supreme over everything and everyone. It's his world, he made it, and he can do with it as he pleases. We may not like his sovereign rule over us, but that doesn't negate the fact that he is the one who reigns supreme over all creation. A good example of this is when God challenges Job with these questions: "Were you there, Job, when I laid the foundations of the earth? Were you there when I measured out the heavens? Were you there when I caused the waters to spring forth like a newborn baby?" (Job 38:4–8, paraphrased). Of course, the answer to all of those questions is no. And the implied meaning is that only God can make those claims; he alone is the Creator. The Bible grounds our understanding of God in his role as Creator and then builds on that foundation with increasing layers of complexity and wonder as he reveals himself throughout the rest of the biblical story.

The creation story is written in a way that demonstrates that the God of the Bible is *unique*. When we read these chapters, we need to keep in mind this wasn't the only creation story in the ancient world. Other cultures told their own stories of how their gods brought about the heavens and the earth. Here are several examples:

- The Babylonian seven clay tablets in cuneiform script known as the *Enuma Elish* tell about gods who came into being through the mingling of fresh water and salt water.

- The *Rig-Veda* of Indian tradition says the world began through "the life force that was covered with emptiness" (10.129), arising through heat and water and desire.[2] The gods that were derived from this life force were created at the same time as the universe.

- The Chinese tell of the giant Pangu, who slept in an egg-shaped darkness. When he awoke and stretched, the egg was broken and fell upward to create the heavens and downward to create the earth, the forces of yin and yang.[3]

When compared to these other ancient creation narratives, something becomes patently clear about the Bible's account of creation. It's different because it introduces us to a completely different kind of God. The creator God of the Bible wasn't created by heat and water. He isn't an impersonal life force or passive actor who was sleeping in eternity. He did not have to strive to create nor was his act of creation accidental. He was not in some cosmic battle against other elements or gods to bring about creation. He existed before creation and he simply spoke the world into existence. No other creation story makes that claim.

The authors of the Old Testament knew that the nations around them had their own gods and their own creation stories. Everything they wrote about God as the Creator was an indictment against those false gods and an inducement for all nations to worship him alone. Psalm 33:8–9 states it plainly, "Let all the earth fear the LORD; let all people of the world revere him. For he spoke, and it came to be; he commanded, and it stood firm."

We might be tempted to think that only the Old Testament talks about God as Creator. That would be a mistake. The New Testament picks up on the theme as well. John 1:1–3 is a striking example: "In the beginning was the Word, and the Word was with God, and the Word was God. He was with God in the beginning. Through him all things were made; without him nothing was made that has been made." The identity of "the Word" in these verses becomes clear when John writes, "The Word became flesh and made his dwelling among us. We have seen his glory, the glory of the one and only Son, who came from the Father, full of grace and truth" (v. 14). The "Word" of John 1:1 is Jesus. He is the creator God incarnate, the God of Genesis 1:1.

The New Testament never makes a distinction between the Creator in Genesis 1 and Jesus. In Colossians 1:15–17, Paul writes, "The Son is the image of the invisible God, the firstborn over all creation. For in him all things were created: things in heaven and on earth, visible and invisible, whether thrones or powers or rulers or authorities; all things have been created through him and for him. He is before all things, and in him all things hold together."

A lot of us who believe in Jesus as Savior don't often think of him as the Creator of the universe. We may even be tempted to think there are discrepancies between the God of the Old Testament and the God of the New Testament. That's one of the problems we face when we don't read the whole Bible as a coherent story. And it's a serious problem. The authors of the New Testament certainly didn't think that way. While delineating the persons of the triune God—Father, Son, and Holy Spirit—they clearly and consistently portray Jesus as the God we read about in the Old Testament. Describing Jesus as Creator is one of the ways they do that.[4]

The grand finale of the Bible, the creation of a new heaven and a new earth in Revelation 21–22, affirms that Jesus is creator God, "the Alpha and the Omega, the Beginning and the End" (21:6). He was the Creator at the beginning, he is the Creator throughout all human history, and he will be the Creator when he brings all of human history to the end he has ordained.

The creation story describes *what* God created, but it doesn't necessarily explain *why* God created the universe. Sometimes we're left to wonder about the answers to questions that the biblical text doesn't answer directly. And that's okay. However, for this latter question if we think of it in light of the big story of the Bible, the answer becomes pretty clear.

We know that God existed before he made everything. He didn't need anything to exist. Therefore, we can assume that God is both eternal and transcendent. He exists outside of time and space. He is not bound by history, geography, the limits of the human intellect, or anything else. But that creates a problem. How can we possibly know a God like that? A God like that cannot be known unless he chooses to reveal himself to us. Creation is the very first act of God revealing himself to us.

When I began to read the Bible as a story, I realized that it narrates from beginning to end how God makes himself known to us. And that changes the way I read the various parts of the Bible. Everything God does in the Bible, even things that make us cringe or things that don't seem to make much sense, he does to make himself known. Why does God create? Because he desires to make himself known. Why does God redeem? He desires to make himself known. We can ask the "why" question about everything we see God doing in the Bible, and the answer will always be the same—he desires to make himself known.

But this raised another question for me. Why does God want to make himself known? Does God's desire to be known imply that he has some unmet need? Does he lack something? Is there some egotistical, self-serving motive that drives him?

No. God needs nothing. When we think about the whole story of the Bible, we see that God makes himself known for our benefit, not for his. Because he makes himself known, we can know him truly. And because he makes himself known, we have the possibility of worshiping him and finding the fullness of life in him. When we blind ourselves to who God truly is, we choose to worship false gods and we choose death.

God's desire to be known springs from his eternal, perfect love. The Father, Son, and Holy Spirit exist eternally in perfect love, joy, and satisfaction. God desires humanity to experience love, joy, and satisfaction in him the way he experiences it in himself. God creates as an act of his love. God redeems as an act of his love. The love of God undergirds the story of the Bible. It lies behind every word, paragraph, chapter, and book.

That might surprise many people today. A lot of folks think the Bible's message is primarily one of judgment and condemnation rather than the story of a loving creator God who desires to be known and worshiped so that we can have the most satisfying life possible. Unfortunately, these folks may have encountered certain Christians whose way of life and relating to them do not communicate a compelling, life-giving picture of a loving God who wants them to know and worship him. Yet, that is the God revealed in the story of the Bible. And that is the story those of us who have believed in Christ have been caught up in. And that changes everything.

The Very Image of God

The creation narrative not only introduces us to our loving, all-powerful Creator, but it also introduces us to ourselves. It doesn't just lay the foundation for our knowledge of God, it also establishes the way we ought to think about ourselves, the way we understand all of humanity in general, and the way we understand life on this earth. When God positions the creation of humanity on the sixth and final day of his creative acts, he communicates that all of his previous handiwork was designed specifically for us.

Once day, several years ago when our children were very young, we were trying to have family devotions at our home. If you have an image of truly obedient children, sitting at my feet waiting breathlessly for the next word to drop from my mouth, you have the wrong idea. Family devotions in our home often degenerated into either discipline or hilarity.

For this particular devotional, my wife and I wanted to stress that God is good. We decided to read through Genesis 1, and every time the word *good* appeared, we would emphasize it by saying it louder than the rest of the text. And so, Genesis 1:10, "God saw that it was good," and then Genesis 1:12, "God saw that it was good." We basically shouted the word *good* every time it appeared in the text.

At the end of the story, we asked our kids, "Why was the creation good?"

They were supposed to say because God is good. However, one of our children, who had an amazing ability to say things that his parents could have never predicted, looked at us and said, "Well duh! It's good because we can live here!"

We didn't see that coming and didn't know how to respond. Needless to say, the rest of that devotional didn't go as planned. Later that day, however, I thought back through the creation narrative, noting how everything God made contributes to just the right environment necessary for the survival of humanity: light, air, water, food. And then I thought about who we are as humans—our finitude and limitations—and it hit me. We could not survive if God hadn't created the earth with exactly the right conditions for us to live in it. So maybe our five-year-old son was right! Maybe the whole creation narrative of days one through five is designed to demonstrate how God, in his love, created a world in which humanity can thrive. He did it all for us. And all creation is good because he seeks our good.

The late American author David Foster Wallace gave the following story in a graduation speech to Kenyon College's class of 2005: "There were these two young fish swimming along and they happen to meet an older fish swimming the other way who nods at them and says, 'Morning boys. How's the water?' The two young fish swim on for a bit and eventually one of them looks over at the other and goes, 'What . . . is water?'" Wallace goes on in the speech to say, "The point of the fish story is merely that the most obvious, important realities are often the ones that are hardest to see and talk about."[5]

Might it be that God's love for us is like water to a fish? He created us and sustains us by his love. Is it possible that even though we are fish in the "water" of God's love, we might not even really recognize that God's creation and sustenance of the world is an act of his love?

The creation narrative progresses purposefully from day one

through day five, building toward the creation of humans on day six as the marvelous climax of God's creative acts. And on that sixth day, in light of all the good things God has created, he makes the extraordinary statement that humanity uniquely is created *as his image*. Let's look carefully at the verses describing day six of creation:

> Then God said, "Let us make mankind in our
> image, in our likeness, so that they may rule over
> the fish in the sea and the birds in the sky, over
> the livestock and all the wild animals, and over
> all the creatures that move along the ground."
> So God created mankind in his own image,
> in the image of God he created them; male and
> female he created them.   (Genesis 1:26–27)

You may have noticed that I used slightly different language to refer to the image of God than the wording found in the text above. I stated that God created humans *as* his image. Most English Bible translations say that God created humanity *in* his image. These different translations, "*in* his image" and "*as* his image," point out subtle but important differences in the way we understand the image of God and humanity.

On the one hand, "in his image" communicates something about *what we are like*. It implies that humans are different from the rest of creation because we possess attributes that are in some small measure like some of God's attributes. On the other hand, "as his image" focuses our attention on what humanity is *created to do*.

During the time when Moses was writing the book of Genesis, kings erected stone images of themselves throughout the lands they conquered. The stone images marked these lands off as the king's possession. They represented his sovereign rule over all who lived within its boundaries. The Hebrew word translated "image" in Genesis 1:27 is the same word used to describe these stone monuments used by the kings. It seems likely that Moses would have used the word with this practice in mind. If that's the case, then we come to the startling conclusion that we are created as the image of God to represent and reveal him as sovereign king over all creation.

We are created with a purpose, a mission that nothing else in creation can fulfill because nothing else was created as God's image. We are created to make God known, to represent and reveal him, throughout all creation. Humans are a direct expression of God's desire that all may know and worship him.[6] In other words, we are made for God's mission. Genesis 1:28 describes how we are to fulfill that mission: "God blessed them and said to them, 'Be fruitful and increase in number; fill the earth and subdue it. Rule over the fish in the sea and the birds in the sky and over every living creature that moves on the ground.'"

Humans, male and female, are given the mandate to be fruitful and multiply and fill the earth with image bearers. Added to that, however, is another mandate—they are also called as God's image to rule over the earth. What a striking command. After God speaks the entire universe into existence and pronounces that it is good, he delegates the authority to govern it to humans. Obviously, God could rule over all creation without us as mediators. But he chose to do it through us. And in all of Scripture, we never learn why.[7]

In the same way, he chose to execute his divine purpose through us. And what is that divine purpose of God? To make himself known to all so that they may worship him and find the fullness of life in him. That's his mission and that's our mission. That is our unique privilege and it provides dignity and worth to us that nothing else in creation bears.

One of the most beautiful places I've ever seen is the area

surrounding Vancouver, British Columbia. After you cross over the Lion's Gate Bridge into West Vancouver you get closer to the mountains. Imagine that we are on the shore of West Vancouver, looking west as the sun sets over Howe Sound. The sky begins to ignite and then explodes in a beautiful array of orange, purple, and red. The beauty of that scene stuns us. And when we turn back to the east to the beautiful Canadian Cascades, we see that same color vibrantly reflected across the majestic snow-covered peaks. This spectacular display of the beauty of God's creation stirs us to praise and worship our Creator. Can you imagine just how beautiful that scene is?

Now imagine that our revelry of wonder and praise to our artistic God is interrupted by an odor. Not too far away from where we are standing, someone has passed out drunk, fallen into the gutter, and vomited all over themselves. Now ask yourself this question: in that entire scene, where is more of God revealed? Is the sun created as the image of God? The spectacular display of color in the heavens? The mountains? The snow? No, none of that is created as the image of God. Only humanity has been created as the image of God. No other part of creation reveals God in the way that humans reveal him. And even though we often choose to live in ways that contradict or even distort the character of our Creator, we are still the only part of creation that bears God's image.

Mike Mason, in his masterful book *The Mystery of Marriage*, captures the uniqueness of humans in relation to the rest of creation: "If man really is fashioned, more than anything else, in the image of God, then clearly it follows that there is nothing on earth so near to God as a human being. The conclusion is inescapable: to be in the presence of even the meanest, lowest, most repulsive specimen of humanity in the world is still to be closer to God than when looking up into a starry sky or at a beautiful sunset."[8]

We are the image of God. Stop and think about that for a moment. I'm pretty adept at focusing on the things that I don't like about myself. I bet you are too. And if we're not careful, we can allow our faults, deficiencies, failures, and sins to define us. But when we dwell there, we're lying to ourselves. Because that's not where our essential identity lies. We are the image of God, uniquely created and commissioned to represent and reveal him throughout all creation. And that's the ultimate foundation of every person's dignity and worth.

One of the reasons our sinfulness is so heinous is because it limits our capacity to fulfill our mission. When we sin, we are choosing to be less than God created us to be, and we are making it more difficult for those around us to know their Creator. In other words, our sins aren't just a personal matter between us and God. They diminish our ability to fulfill God's mission to be known by all.

That's why we have to be remade, born again, through the gospel of Jesus Christ, who himself is described as "the image of the invisible God" (Colossians 1:15). In Christ we are a new creation, and through the regeneration of the Spirit we regain our capacity to reveal the one true God as his image—not perfectly yet, sometimes not even consistently, but more and more as we grow in our faith in Christ.

Made to Worship

But there's something else that sets us apart from the rest of creation. Not only are we uniquely created as the image of God, we are also uniquely created to relate to God in a way that nothing else in creation can. We are made to worship.[9]

Genesis 2:7 reveals something more about the way we have been created. It shows that we are not only made alive *by* God, but we are made alive *to* God: "Then the LORD God formed a man from the dust of the ground and breathed into his nostrils the breath of life, and the man became a living being." Only the creation of humans is described in this way. Only humans are animated by God breathing "the breath of life" into them. In this verse, the Hebrew term translated "the breath of life" (*neshamah*) is used in the Bible only for God and for humanity. In other words, only humans and God possess the *neshamah*.[10] In some mysterious yet very real way, we are alive in a way that no other living creature is alive. We are spiritually alive and able to relate to God like nothing else. We are more alive than anything else in creation because we have experienced the animation of our souls. We are truly and wholly alive, made to connect with God at the deepest level. We are made to worship. Wow. Stop and let that sink in for a moment.

And not only that. Because we have the *neshamah*, we also have the unique capacity to make moral decisions that express our spiritually alive souls. We are made to obey. Proverbs 20:27 says, "The human spirit [*neshamah*] is like the lamp of the LORD, searching all his innermost parts" (NET). In this verse, *neshamah* "functions as a conscience, enabling people to know and please God, and directing them in choices that will be life-giving."[11] Not only are we made alive spiritually so that we can worship God in relationship with him, our consciences are also made alive so that we can make moral decisions that please him.

But there's even more to being made alive spiritually so that we can live in relationship with our Creator. We are also made to work. Genesis 2:15 says, "The LORD God took the man and put him in the Garden of Eden to work it and take care of it." The Hebrew verbs in this passage translated "work" and "take care of" are related to language used later in the Old Testament to describe the service of the priests in the temple of the Lord. The use of these terms in the creation narrative implies that all of creation ought to be seen as God's temple and that humanity's work in creation is like the service priests rendered to God as they worshiped in the temple.[12]

The connection between the temple of God and the garden of Eden is powerful because both are described as places of God's presence. For instance, when the Israelites finished building the temple in Jerusalem and placed the ark of the covenant in it, the glory of the Lord filled the temple (1 Kings 8:1–11). This theme continues in the New Testament when Paul writes to the church in Corinth, "Don't you know that you yourselves are God's temple and that God's Spirit dwells in your midst?" (1 Corinthians 3:16). The creation of the first humans in the garden of Eden begins this powerful reality of living in relationship with God, worshiping God, revealing God, and serving God in creation. Humans are uniquely created and animated to do just that.

Made for Each Other

The creation narrative ends with an idyllic picture of the life enjoyed by the first humans in the garden of Eden. Having already stated categorically that both man and woman are created as God's image, the narrative goes on in Genesis 2:18–22 to describe why and how God created the woman. Being written in a place and time when women were considered to be inferior to men and often treated as if they were little more than possessions of the men in their families, this passage makes the bold statement that women are equal to men in every way and necessary partners in the fulfillment of the mandate given to humans as image bearers. Eve is an image bearer, animated by the "breath of life," and uniquely suited to participate with Adam in the mission of filling the earth with image bearers.

Adam and Eve come together as equals, uniquely created to form the one-flesh union that will become the basis of human civilization. Theirs is indeed a "blessed alliance."[13] And they enjoy one another with unabashed joy and satisfaction. They are "both naked, and ... felt no shame" (Genesis 2:25). They have everything they could possibly need to fulfill their mandate to represent, worship, and live in relationship with their Creator. They breathe his good breath and they reveal his good attributes. They live in his presence in perfect harmony with all creation and in perfect union with one another. They are completely and wholly engaged in enjoying the good creation God has made for them.

I love watching our grandchildren enjoy a new playground. They run, climb, slide, and swing. At times they might stop to pick up and examine bits of mulch or fistfuls of sand. They are completely absorbed in the fun and wonder of this new place to play. Aware of nothing other than the things they are touching, seeing, and doing, they don't seem to have a care in the world.

That's the image of Adam and Eve that we find at the end of the creation narrative. Life is good and they are completely satisfied with it. They are fully and wholly alive. And they are unaware of any danger, even naive to the possibility that anything could threaten their happiness.

The very next verse of the Bible, however, shatters their naivete. There is a predator lurking in the garden whose desire is to destroy them: "Now the serpent was more crafty than any of the wild animals the LORD God had made" (Genesis 3:1). The tone of the narrative darkens. For the first time, we feel tension and uncertainty.

What happens next changes everything.

4

FALL

Google estimates that more than 130 million books have been published over the course of human history.[1] Which means this book somehow had to attract your attention out of a multitude of new releases, familiar bestsellers, and great classics of literature.

Why did you pick this particular book out of all the possible choices? I suspect your choice had far more to do with the book this book is about! There is no other book like the Bible. Nothing else even comes close. And that's why it is the bestselling book of all time with more than six billion copies sold. No other book has influenced the Western world like the Bible. No other book has inspired and captivated people like the Bible. No other book has the words of eternal life. No other book. Just the Bible.

In 2017, book sales in the United States exceeded $1.8 billion. Topping the list of bestselling genres, not surprisingly for our educated country, is textbooks. Near the end of that list, in ninth place out of ten was the genre "Arts and Photography."[2] Now, I love paging through a beautiful photo journal. The individuals who create these glossy, oversized books show us our galaxy, our planet, and our humanity in breathtaking ways we simply can't see on our own.

But even though I love that kind of book, I can't tell you the last time I purchased one. In fact, these books circulate poorly in our libraries[3] and have been largely relegated to used book shops and wholesale club store shelves. Maybe that's because these books typically don't tell a story. They don't necessarily engage us with the critical features of a story like structure, crisis, climax, and resolution.

What Happened in That Garden?

In its first two chapters the Bible paints some lovely pictures. The creation narrative evokes images of beautiful forests, lakes, animals, birds, seas, and sky in the good heavens and earth God created. But the Bible doesn't just give us a series of beautiful pictures in these chapters. By the time God gives the first humans their mandate, there's already a sense of drama and purpose on the pages. There's purpose in the mandate itself and tension in the question of how humans, male and female, will fulfill it. There's tension when we see that the man cannot fulfill the mandate alone. And then there's resolution when God creates the woman so that together they can fill the earth and rule over it as his image bearers.

But the whole Bible develops an even bigger narrative from this foundational creation account. Something happens within and to that creation. Somehow, we get from creation in Genesis 1:1, "In the beginning God created the heavens and the earth," to "I am making everything new!" in Revelation 21:5. The pages in between these two statements aren't like a coffee table book of beautiful scenes. They tell a story.

Something happened in the garden of Eden that created the need for God to intervene and engage with creation in a way that would allow him to fulfill his desire that all people worship him alone and enjoy the fullness of life in him alone. The ultimate fulfillment of that desire is the vivid portrayal of the new heaven and new earth near the end of the book of Revelation.

But what happened in the garden? If we don't take the time to fully understand the shocking events described in Genesis 3, the rest of the Bible won't make much sense. If you had not read the Bible before and came to the end of Genesis 2, you would never expect what happens next. Adam and Eve rebel against the wishes of their Creator, the one who had given them everything they could ever possibly need. Theologians call their act of rebellion the "fall of humanity." In story language this is the *inciting incident,* the scene that completely disorders the setting and its characters, catches the reader off guard, raises tension, and changes the expected arc of the story.

The Bible never flinches in describing how Adam's and Eve's sin affects humanity. It is not a PG story; at places it's a PG-13 or even an R-rated story. The Bible is a story that causes us to ask hard questions about ourselves and forces us to come to grips with the effects of human rebellion. The Bible reveals to us just how far we've fallen from what God created us to be and how thoroughly we have compromised our capacity to be his image.

The fall of humanity in Genesis 3 starts with temptation, continues with rebellion, and then concludes with God's response to that rebellion. The narrative catches us off guard. None of it is expected. We don't expect a serpent in the garden who opposes its Creator. We don't expect the humans to rebel against their Creator. And we could never anticipate God's response. We need to pay close attention, however, because his response to human defiance and rebellion is repeated throughout the Bible. It forms the theological foundation of redemption.

First, let's dig a little deeper into the rebellion that causes the first humans to lose the unique relationship they have with their

Creator and causes creation itself to become far less than God designed it to be.

A Predator in the Garden

The description of Adam and Eve at the end of Genesis 2 reads, "Adam and his wife were both naked, and they felt no shame" (v. 25). The language in this verse is evocative. "Naked" implies that the man and the woman had a sense of innocence before their Creator and before each other. But their innocence may also have included a measure of naivete. In other words, they felt no threat of danger in the "good" creation they enjoyed. Like children on a playground, they were completely consumed with enjoying the good things God had created for them and doing the good work he had given them to do. They had no fear that anything evil even existed much less that they were in danger of falling prey to it.

That understanding is further developed by the phrase "they felt no shame." Shame in this context means far more than simply embarrassment. It implies that they did not fear being exploited or harmed because they innocently believed that God's good creation contained no one who would seek to harm them. It's as if they were unaware of any possibility of evil, unwilling to allow themselves to think that anything could go wrong. But, indeed, their innocence is quickly exposed as naivete. A predator lurked in the garden whose intent was to do them harm.

Genesis 3:1 introduces that threat, "Now the serpent was more crafty than any of the wild animals the LORD God had made." There's a Hebrew wordplay between the words translated "crafty" (*arum*) in this verse and "naked" (*arom*) in the previous verse.[4] The wordplay emphasizes that their innocence makes them perfect prey for the serpent's craftiness. The Hebrew word translated as "crafty" in this verse can also mean "prudent" or "clever" when used in a positive sense. Here it is clearly negative.[5] The basic idea is that a crafty person knows what to do to accomplish what they want. If their desires are negative or harmful, that person can be described as "cunning" or "crafty." If their desires are positive and helpful, they can be called "clever" or "prudent." Clearly the serpent's intent in this passage is to do harm.

If we were moviegoers, we could envision a similar scene from a movie. Imagine a backyard barbecue on a beautiful, late-summer day. The adults are engaged in lighthearted conversation, flipping sizzling burgers, enjoying frosty drinks. Their children are joyfully playing soccer on the perfectly manicured lawn at the edge of a thick forest. The musical score is breezy and cheery and the scene is full of light. But in the middle of all the friendly banter and innocent play, the film's tone changes and the music modulates into a minor key.

Tension rises. We feel anxious as the landscape turns dark and ominous. The camera pans to a dangerous-looking man lurking in the trees just beyond the yard. He is watching the children play, shifting his eyes to note the inattention of the laughing adults. As he sneaks through the trees with his gaze fixed on the kids, we know that he is a threat and our sense of dread grows. With a wayward kick, the soccer ball rolls past the children and slows near the trees where the man stands in the shadows. One child calls out, "I'll get it!" and the closeup shows the man focusing his narrowed eyes on that child. The adults are oblivious. The threat is real. The music grows more intense. As you view the scene, your pulse increases and you grip the arms of your chair. Can you picture that scene and feel your response to it? That's exactly the way we should read the end of Genesis 2 and the beginning of chapter 3.

After the serpent is introduced the story unfolds quickly. In the midst of this perfect garden and the couple's perfect relationships with one another and with God, the serpent is able to tempt Eve with lies that become the foundation for all human sin. He says in effect, "There might be something even more satisfying than the good life God has created for you. God is holding something back that would give you an even better life. God is stingy and doesn't want you to fully enjoy all that this world has to offer. In fact, God is keeping you from becoming divine like him" (Genesis 3:1–5 paraphrased).

The serpent's lies impugn God's character, mischaracterize God's desires for us, and pervert the nature of God's relationship with us. And these lies come directly from one who embodies the very presence of evil. One who opposes God at every turn, Satan himself, the chief of all liars. Jesus reminded those who opposed him that they were just like their father, the devil, who "has always hated the truth, because there is no truth in him. When he lies, it is consistent with his character; for he is a liar and the father of lies" (John 8:44 NLT).

The tension in the narrative mounts. Do you feel it when you read these verses? What will the woman do? Will she believe the lies of the serpent as he twists God's words and intent? That's the power of reading Scripture as a story. It humanizes the text, draws us in emotionally, and heightens our anticipation for what's coming next.

Tragically, the serpent's cunning deception leads Eve to believe that God has, indeed, held something back and there is a life better than the good life God has given them in the garden. Genesis 3:6 describes Adam's and Eve's stunning betrayal of their Creator: "When the woman saw that the fruit of the tree was good for food and pleasing to the eye, and also desirable for gaining wisdom, she took some and ate it. She also gave some to her husband, who was with her, and he ate it."

The serpent's lies stir desires in them that they had never experienced before. But they didn't have to give in to them. After all, they have been given authority over every living creature and have received a mandate to work and protect God's good creation. They could simply command the serpent to be silent and slither away. But they don't. They want more than the life God has given them. They want to usurp God's place and become gods themselves. So they eat. And everything changes. Everything.

The Rebellion

As described in Genesis 2:9, two special trees grew in the middle of the garden of Eden, the tree of life and the tree of the knowledge of good and evil. God prohibited Adam and Eve from eating fruit from the tree of the knowledge of good and evil, but he did not prohibit them from eating the fruit that grew on the tree of life. Evidently, eating fruit from this tree was life-giving. Rather than see it as fruit that granted immediate immortality, it is likely that eating the fruit from this tree extended life. Thus, if the humans ate regularly from the tree of life, they would live as long as they had access to it. But eating fruit from the tree of the knowledge of good and evil, the one God explicitly forbade them to eat from, had the exact opposite effect. It didn't give life; it brought death.

When Eve and Adam give in to the temptation to willfully disobey their Creator, the trajectory of the story arcs in a wholly different direction. When they eat from the tree of the knowledge of good and evil, they don't just eat a piece of fruit; they partake in evil itself. Genesis 3:7 tells us, "Then the eyes of both of them were opened, and they realized they were naked." Perfection disappears. Innocence shatters. Relationships rupture. Their naivete toward evil is obliterated. They are now fully aware of good and evil. Fully aware that they have chosen evil. And the die is cast for all of us.

We call their sin "the fall of humanity," and the resulting human condition after their rebellion "human depravity." These terms are not directly present in the language of Genesis 3, but they are widely used to describe humanity's rebellion against God, an ongoing defiance that we see in the rest of Scripture and in our own lives.

But what does all of this mean for you and me today? Setting aside the questions about the effect of Adam and Eve's rebellion on all humanity that theologians have debated for centuries, let's just think about what we can see in the story and in our own lives.

Adam and Eve were created with the ability to make moral choices. So are we. They freely chose to defy God's command and disobey. So do we. The story of the Bible makes it painfully clear that there are no morally innocent people. We all sin because we choose to do so. At various points in our lives, we all believe the lie that God is holding back something from us that would make our lives so much better. And we all choose to believe that we know better than God how we should live.

The language we often use to talk about sin masks the reality that we willfully choose to disobey God on a daily basis. For example, we talk about "falling" into sin. That makes it seem like what we do is accidental. What if we change the metaphor and talk about jumping into sin or running after evil? The truth is, that's what we do. I will never forget the day this harsh reality hit me full force.

In the late 1980s my wife and I and our children were living in Kraków, Poland, less than fifty miles from the infamous Nazi concentration camp, Auschwitz. It is estimated that of the 1.3 million men, women, and children sent to the camp between 1940 and 1945, 1.1 million of them died. Ninety percent of those who died were Jews. I had read those statistics but they were just numbers until the day I walked under the hideous, mocking German phrase *"Arbeit macht frei"* ("Work makes you free") above the iron gates of Auschwitz.

The visit began with a documentary containing film clips of life in the camp that had been shot by the Nazis for propaganda purposes. They were proud of the way Auschwitz brought them closer to the "Final Solution," the extermination of the Jewish race. The images in the film shocked and saddened me. Then I walked through several of the buildings, originally used as Polish army barracks, that had been converted into displays depicting some of the realities of life in the camp. I looked upon piles of personal items taken from people when they were processed as prisoners into the camp—shoes, hats, coats, suitcases, canes, hairbrushes, toothbrushes, eyeglasses, children's toys, even prosthetic limbs. I walked through rooms with tightly packed wooden shelves where straw mattresses and filthy rags served as beds and I peered into tiny solitary confinement cells. I also saw the wall where prisoners were executed by firing squads, clinics where they were subjected to medical experiments like lab rats, and the "showers" where tens of thousands were gassed with the deadly Zyklon B. And finally, I saw the ovens where the bodies were cremated for quick and easy disposal.

It was all chillingly efficient, so well designed and engineered. Walking back out of the camp I was overwhelmed with the realization that Auschwitz was not the site of a crime of passion or momentary insanity. It was an example of the human capacity to design, build, and execute an efficient process to accomplish a goal. Auschwitz was a brilliantly engineered factory designed to mass-produce death.

I asked myself, "Who has the capacity for that kind of evil?"

"I do."

And I threw up.

And the idea that we "fall" into sin was forever erased from my mind.

Before the serpent ever tempted Adam and Eve to disobey, God had already told them what the outcome would be if they did so. In Genesis 2:16–17, he said, "You are free to eat from any tree in the garden; but you must not eat from the tree of the knowledge of good and evil, for when you eat from it you will certainly die." The penalty for their rebellion is clear. Justice demands that they be barred from the tree of life and surely die. Death is the penalty for rebellion against God. Always has been. Always will be. That's why the apostle Paul describes us as being dead in our transgressions and sins (Ephesians 2:1).

Adam's and Eve's sin corrupts every relationship. It ruptures their relationships with God, their relationship with one another, and their relationships with the good creation God had graciously given them.[6] Their joyous intimacy is replaced by shame. They hide from one another underneath coverings they make for themselves. Guilt floods their consciences and they hide from their Creator in the good creation that he had given them.

Now what?

Once again, the story takes us to a place of tense uncertainty. What is God going to do? Has his desire that all creation know and worship him been thwarted by human rebellion? Is he going to be done with these humans and just start over?[7]

God's Response

If you had never read this story before, you would be on the edge of your seat wondering what God is going to do in the face of Adam's and Eve's open defiance. Pay close attention here because God's initial response isn't what we expect. It is a response that we will see again and again throughout the story of the Bible. God responds to human rebellion with justice, mercy, and grace. He did so when the first humans sinned and he has done so ever since.

Several years ago, I heard Stuart Briscoe, longtime pastor of Elmbrook Church in Brookfield, Wisconsin, describe the relationship between God's justice, grace. Recalling a conversation he had with one of his children, he said, "Justice gives you what deserve. Mercy does not give you all you deserve. Grace gives you what you don't deserve."[8]

Briscoe's description is helpful and I think it's well worth our time to unpack it a bit. Because of his *justice*, God always judges sin. We get what we deserve. We deserve to bear the consequences of our sin. When God judges our sin, however, he restrains its destructive power in our lives and in the lives of others. Because of his *mercy*, God forbears the full extent of the penalty that we deserve and gives us an opportunity to repent. And because of his *grace*, God gives us what we don't deserve. He forgives our sin and restores us to relationship with him. Let's explore how each of these responses guide the narrative in Genesis 3.

FIRST, JUSTICE. Genesis 3:8 reads, "Then the man and his wife heard the sound of the LORD God as he was walking in the garden in the cool of the day, and they hid from the LORD God among the trees of the garden." I have heard preachers and others talk about this verse in this way: "Well, God had a habit of walking with Adam and Eve in the garden every day, so this is just his normal daily stroll." This approach creates in our minds an image that God's response to Adam's and Eve's rebellion is rather casual. Is God just out for a leisurely stroll in the garden on a cool afternoon completely unaware of what just happened? Or is he disinterested in their disobedience?

Would the one who created Adam and Eve, the one who gave them a moral conscience and commanded them to obey, just respond to their rebellion by going through his normal daily routine? God is never casual about sin. Never. God's justice explodes in the narrative. He enters the garden in a way that demonstrates he will always judge sin.

When we read that they heard the "sound" of the Lord God,

it reminds us of the occasions in the Old Testament when the people heard the sound (translated "voice" in many passages) of God, and they "trembled" in fear (for example, Exodus 20:18). In fact, the author of Hebrews reminds his readers that the Lord's voice "shook the earth" and made those assembled at the foot of Mount Sinai tremble in fear (Hebrews 12:18–21, 25–27). So the sound of the Lord God entering the garden here isn't the sound of carefree footsteps on a mossy, leaf-laden pathway, but a sound that brings a sense of terror and the fear of judgment.

Let's also look at the word translated "walking" in Genesis 3:8. The Hebrew verb can be used in a more general sense to imply movement.[9] Therefore, this part of the verse could be translated, "They heard the sound of the Lord God moving into the garden." If you've ever been hiking in a forest when a storm is approaching, you know that you can hear a powerful wind before you ever feel it. The additional phrase in verse 8, "in the cool of the day," is a translation built around the Hebrew word which often means "wind." It refers to that time of the day when the wind picks up and cools the air.

Think about the image created by most English translations of verse 8. Most of us think of God casually walking in the garden. But what if we change the translation to "and the Lord God *moved into* the garden in the *sound of the wind*." And I don't think it was a gentle breeze. Psalm 29 and Job 38 both describe the Lord moving in the *roar* of the wind. Both of those chapters use similar language to Genesis 3:8.[10]

This sound of the Lord is more than just the rustling of leaves. Here is a holy God confronting human rebellion in a howling wind of judgment.[11] That's why Adam and Eve hide. They know they have rebelled against God. They know the penalty for their disobedience. They know he has come to judge them. They hide because they are afraid that they are going to die as punishment for their sin. We know what God has said he will do, but the narrative at this point gives us a moment to live in the tension of wondering, "What is God going to do?" He has come in judgment. But what comes next?

NEXT, MERCY. The answer takes my breath away. In a completely unexpected twist in the story, God responds to their rebellion with a seemingly silly question not a thundering condemnation: "But the Lord God called to the man, 'Where are you?'" (Genesis 3:9). Does God know where the man is? Of course he knows! But by posing the question, God is inviting Adam to stop hiding and *to approach* him. God doesn't roar into the garden, pronounce judgment, and execute the sinner. When God comes into the garden in judgment, he invites Adam and Eve *to step back toward him.* That's mercy. Shocking and undeserved.

The same scenario plays out as God questions Adam and Eve in verses 11–13. Again, these questions do not betray a lack of knowledge on God's part. Instead, they reveal the seriousness of the rebellion. Each question reveals God's willingness to restrain condemnation for their sin and to give them an opportunity to repent.

Let's be sure to avoid two mistakes in thinking about God's mercy. First, we must never separate God's mercy and his justice. God always judges sin, and the penalties of his justice are real. Second, we must not see God's judgment as just an act of doom and retribution. God's response to sin is never driven by a need to get even but by his desire that humans find the fullness of life in knowing and worshiping him. Throughout the Bible when God announces judgment, he is issuing an invitation to step back into a relationship with him. That's God's mercy. Even though God has invited Adam and Eve to step back into relationship with him, that relationship will never be the same. They will bear consequences for their sin. Their relationship with God has been compromised, and the repercussions of their sin will plague all of humanity from this point forward. Cut off from the tree of life, they will surely die. In this way, they have died. And so have we. Through Adam's rebellion, sin and death entered the world and became the reality for every human who has ever lived (Romans 5:12–13).

The life God created for Adam and Eve in the garden has now vanished. The life-giving, ever-present relationship they enjoyed with God has been compromised, and life itself will now be characterized by struggle, strife, fear, and the ever-present specter of death. God's justice demands that there will be consequences for their sin, but his mercy demonstrates that he has not totally abandoned them. God pronounces these consequences and they are severe, but he will make provision for them. And that is God's grace.

THE TRAGIC CONSEQUENCES OF SIN. Genesis 3:14–24 describes how Adam and Eve will bear the consequences of their rebellion. It is interesting to note that they are not cursed, but the serpent and the land are cursed. The serpent is doomed. Although he will strike and strive to destroy God's image bearers, the serpent's fate is certain and, in the end, he will be destroyed (Genesis 3:14–15). The curse upon the land means that God's favor has been removed from it. Instead of freely giving of its bounty, the earth will yield its goodness only through the painful toil of the humans.

The man and the woman will experience essentially the same punishment for their sin.[12] Their relationship with God has been severed, and their ability to fulfill the purpose for which they were created—to be fruitful, multiply, fill the earth with the image of God, and rule over creation—is now in doubt. Before their rebellion, the privilege of fulfilling the creation mandate—bearing children and causing the earth to bring forth its bounty—would have contained no uncertainty. That was God's promise. It was the means whereby God would accomplish his will to be known throughout all creation and a promise of his abiding, sustaining presence in their lives.

Instead, the woman's life will be characterized by fear and uncertainty as she bears children. We should not assume that childbirth would have been painless had Adam and Eve not rebelled against God. Human anatomy and the physical realities of pregnancy and childbirth make that highly unlikely. Pain in childbirth isn't the issue. The question is whether the woman and child will survive the trauma of the birthing process without God's abiding and sustaining presence (Genesis 3:16).

I will never forget the births of our three children. Even living at the time in a country with excellent medical care, the trauma and pain that my wife experienced during labor and delivery terrified me. And I had the easy part! Childbirth can be dangerous especially for those without access to adequate medical facilities and care. The World Health Organization estimates that more than eight hundred women per day died from complications related to childbirth in 2017.[13] Eve, like all women after her, would experience that pain and trauma without the assurance that she and the child would survive. Such were the awful consequences of Adam's and Eve's rebellion.

Furthermore, strife in the relationship between the man and the woman also created uncertainty about whether they would be able to fill the earth with image bearers now that their union with one another has been compromised. The very relationship through which the man and woman would fulfill the mandate given to them in the garden, the one-flesh union of man and woman in marriage, is now brought into question. The man's life will also be characterized by the loss of certainty that he will be able to carry out the mandate to protect and tend the garden.[14] Even though he will work the earth with painful toil, there is no certainty that it will yield its life-giving sustenance. Everything has changed for them because their relationship with the Creator has been compromised by their sin.

Toil, pain, and uncertainty in their labors will characterize the striving of the man and the woman to fulfill their mandate as humans. The teacher in Ecclesiastes sums up the futility of life after humanity's relationship with the Creator is severed: "What do people get for all the toil and anxious striving with which they labor under the sun? All their days their work is grief and pain; even at night their minds do not rest. This too is meaningless" (Ecclesiastes 2:22–23).

Although a life of fear and futility is a severe consequence of sin, the greatest punishment that Adam and Eve experience is banishment from the garden and from a blessed life of unending satisfaction; they lose access to the tree of life and to God himself (Genesis 3:22–24). This loss creates the certainty of death, a certainty that plagues every human being from that point forward regardless of race, citizenship, wealth, education, intelligence, and health. Everyone dies. "The overwhelming loss was not paradise; it was God. Throughout the rest of the Old Testament one never hears talk of regaining the comfort of Eden, but regaining access to God's presence was paramount."[15]

Finally, Grace, and a Glimpse of Redemption. But God wasn't finished with his image bearers. As the narrative unfolds, we continue to see not only his justice and mercy but also his grace. Adam and Eve had done nothing to merit God's favor, yet he intervenes on their behalf so that they can continue to fulfill their mandate and find some satisfaction in the life God is now giving them.

In Genesis 3:19, Adam names the woman "Eve," a Hebrew term that likely means "living."[16] The text explains that the woman received this name "because she would become the mother of all the living" (v. 20). Although Adam and Eve will surely die, that does not mean the end of humanity. God promised that they will bear children. And when Eve gives birth to a son, she exclaims, "With the help of the LORD I have brought forth a 'human'" (Genesis 4:1; paraphrase). That is God's grace.

Another act of God's grace is the clothing that he provides for Adam and Eve to cover their nakedness (Genesis 3:21). After they sin, they attempt to cover themselves with fig leaves because they have become aware of their alienation from one another and their shame before God. But God provides more than fig leaves to cover their nakedness; he gives them coverings made from animal skins (Genesis 3:21). These more substantial coverings signal that the world they will enter outside the garden is more threatening than anything they have experienced. The clothing God makes for them will be needed for them to survive outside the garden. It's not just an act to comfort them in their insecurity but an action to preserve their lives.

And the humans survive. As the story of Adam and Eve's descendants unfolds, we see that God's justice, mercy, and grace have their intended effect. They bear more children. They raise crops and tend flocks. They offer sacrifices to God. They build cities and develop arts and tools. Ultimately, we read, "At that time people began to call on the name of the LORD" (Genesis 4:26). That is how God's justice, mercy, and grace work; they lead us to know and worship him.

God's response to human rebellion—justice, mercy, and grace—is the basis of redemption. We see it repeatedly in the early chapters of Genesis. We see it when God sends Cain into exile with a mark of protection instead of killing him for the sin of murdering his own brother. We see it when God doesn't wipe out all of humanity but makes a way for the human race to continue through the provision of an ark in which Noah's family and representatives survive the flood. We see it when God judges the sin of the people of Babel by scattering them and restoring them to their mandate to "fill the earth." When we see, even in the earliest chapters of the Bible, the pattern of God's response to human rebellion—justice, mercy, and grace—we are seeing the foundation of God's redemptive mission, a preview of the central story arc of the Bible.

What a start to the story! The opening scenes take us to heights of elation, plunge us into the depths of despair, and jerk us around plot twists and turns that we can't see coming. Through it all we see the power and love of God, the sinister presence of evil, the willful rebellion of humans, and the tragic consequences of sin. God's response to their rebellion—justice, mercy, and grace—simply takes our breath away. The rest of the Bible doesn't make sense unless we have a grip on how these opening chapters set up the rest of the story.

So let's get to it! The rest of the story is just as beautiful, surprising, and powerful as the parts we've looked at so far.

5

REDEMPTION IN THE OLD TESTAMENT

loved reading to our kids when they were young. Sitting on the bed, leaned back against the headboard, snuggled close to one another, reading one of our family favorites—parenting doesn't get much better than that. We read a lot of great books together, but I think J. R. R. Tolkien's *The Lord of the Rings* was the clear family favorite. Evidently, we're not alone in that assessment. With more than 150 million copies sold worldwide, it ranks as one of the bestselling novels of all time. What an amazing story. Fantastical creatures, lovable and despicable characters, massive battles, harrowing escapes, terrifying enemies, intrigue, suspense—all on an epic scale—and an unlikely hero. What's not to like about a story like that?

Yes, there are a lot of reasons to like *The Lord of the Rings*. First and foremost, however, it's a redemption story and we love redemption stories. One of the most commonly crafted kinds of stories in all of literature, they all unfold in basically the same way: life is good, evil comes, people are in peril, rescue is needed, a hero intervenes, evil is defeated, the main characters are rescued, and the good life is restored. That's a redemption story. How many movies have that basic plot structure? Hundreds? Thousands? How many novels are based on the same basic story arc? Redemption stories transcend generations and cultures.

Could it be that the story of redemption has been written on the hearts of humans by God himself?

The Bible is a redemption story, pure and simple. It has fascinating characters, battles, escapes, enemies, surprises, intrigue, suspense, and an unlikely hero. All of these elements are woven together into the most epic, most compelling redemption story ever told. It begins with the creation of an ideal world where life is to be lived to the fullest. The first humans live in perfect fellowship with their Creator. They lack nothing. But evil tempts them to rebel against their Creator and they do so. Sin, death, and evil plague humanity. Humans cannot free themselves from the consequences of their rebellion. Someone has to intervene to rescue them from their plight and restore them to the life God created for them. They need a hero. They need redemption.

Getting Our Terms Right

Sometimes we use words not really knowing what they mean. That can be especially true of "churchy" words like *justification* and *sanctification*. We hear them all the time, but we may have a hard time explaining what they mean to folks who aren't in church on a regular basis. Another of our favorite churchy words is *redemption*. And here's the great thing about that one. Because of the prevalence of redemption stories in the broader culture, most folks have likely heard that word and have some vague sense of what it means. It's a great starting place to help someone understand what the Bible is all about.

That's what I needed while trying to answer my seatmate's question on that flight out of Paris when he pointed at my Bible and asked, "What is that book about?" I needed a starting point that he could relate to. But because I hadn't yet begun to read the Bible as a story, I flailed around, throwing in a lot of churchy words that didn't make a lot of sense to him. If only I had just told him the story, he may have come up with redemption on his own.

Having lived overseas for a number of years and learning to speak two languages beyond my native English, I know how difficult it can be to create genuine understanding when we communicate with one another. Sometimes the words we use create more confusion than understanding.

My wife and I moved to Vienna, Austria, just after we were married in the early 1980s. During that time, we traveled and ministered in countries throughout the Soviet bloc. Then, we moved to Poland near the end of the Communist era. We didn't speak Polish and started in language lessons right away. It was a tough time in Poland. Political unrest and a faltering economy led to frequent shortages of fuel, food, and other consumer goods. The basic rule was, if you see something in the shop, buy it. That meant we lived in a kind of hunter-gatherer mode. Just about every day after my language courses at the university, I would walk a circuit of several shops just to see what might be available.

One day, I saw what looked like a plucked rubber chicken in a shop window. Fresh meat was only in the shops from time to time, and we'd had difficulty finding it. I walked closer, passing by the long line of people waiting to get in the door, and saw an unfamiliar word on the front of the shop that I thought must mean "poultry" because of the plucked rubber chicken in the window. I quickly joined the back of the long line with visions of taking a chicken home to the family. Since it looked like it was going to take a while to get my prized chicken, I decided to take this opportunity to practice my very limited Polish with the folks standing in line.

As we got into the shop, the folks near me continued to be amused with my infantile conversational skills. Unfortunately, that meant I was oblivious to what had been going on inside. So, when I found myself face-to-face with the sales lady behind the counter, she reminded me in a very disapproving tone that I was actually there to shop and not to entertain. At least, that's what it seemed like she said. I made my request, "I would like a chicken." At this she chided me with a very long and very loud sentence that did not result in her giving me a chicken.

So, in my best Polish, not having understood anything that she said, I asked again for a chicken. At which point, in frustration, she reached under the counter, cut off a block of cheese and handed it to me. I looked at the cheese, knowing full well it wasn't a chicken and attempted to communicate to her that I, in fact, wanted a chicken. In an even louder voice, she said something close to what she'd said before, though I still didn't understand it. Knowing that I was defeated, I simply held out my money in the other hand, and she took what must have been the value of the cheese. I left the store, having gone in to buy a chicken and leaving with a block of cheese.

I knew I'd used the correct word for chicken. One of the very first things we learned in language school was how to buy a chicken in the market. I thought I'd said it the right way, yet I walked out of the store with cheese. I had no idea why things had gone so wrong. I later learned from a friend that the word on the front of the shop meant "dairy." I walked out of that store with a block of cheese instead of a chicken because I was in a shop that sold dairy products. (I'm still not sure why there was a plucked rubber chicken in the shop window.)

I needed an interpreter in that shop, someone who understood the context and the language well enough to help me understand what was going on. I'm afraid a lot of folks feel the same way when it comes to reading the Bible. Let's face it, there are a lot of unfamiliar words in the Bible, not to mention a ton of strange-sounding names, bizarre behaviors, and confounding events. That's why we need to be able to step back from the details and explain the big story of the Bible in a way that at least sounds familiar to folks. *Redemption* is the key. It's the best word to summarize the big story of the Bible. It's the best word to describe how God engages humanity from start to finish.

We need to take a deep dive into redemption. Otherwise, we won't be able to understand what the Bible is all about.

Another Turning Point in the Story

We've already seen in the first eleven chapters of the Bible that God responds to human rebellion with justice, mercy, and grace. He does so with Adam and Eve, Cain, Noah, and the people who built the Tower of Babel. In each case God judges sin, mercifully gives people an opportunity to repent, and graciously allows them to return to him. But at the end of Genesis 11, there is still a lot of doubt about how God is going to accomplish his mission to be known and worshiped by all. Humanity's proclivity to constant rebellion against their Creator seems unstoppable. What is God going to do to accomplish his mission?

In Genesis 12:1–3, we find the surprising answer to that question. God chooses one man from the diverse, multitudinous, and rebellious nations described in the story up to this point. He's a rather obscure person who hasn't figured into the story at all. Yet, God called this man and chose him to be the one through whom he would make himself known to all. That man was Abraham.[1]

God's call and promises to Abraham form another pivot point in the story of the Bible. Through Abraham, God promises to create a nation for himself, a people who will worship him and will make him known to all peoples.[2] Known later in the story as the nation of Israel, the descendants of Abraham will be

God's chosen people, and he will be their God. Through this nation, God will show the world what redemption means. They will come to describe themselves as "the redeemed" and their God as "the one who redeems."

In order to explore what redemption means in the Bible, we have to explore how God relates to his people, the descendants of Abraham.

RESCUE. In the summer of 2018, we were captivated by the international effort to rescue twelve young boys and their twenty-five-year-old assistant soccer coach from a flooded cave in the Chiang Rai province of Thailand. The boys had been trapped in a complex of caves by unexpectedly heavy monsoon rains that filled the underground passage with water, making it impossible for them to get out. After nine days of searching, rescuers found them stranded on a ledge, 2.5 miles from the cave entrance. It would be another five days before the rescue effort could begin in earnest. Altogether that endeavor would require more than ten thousand people including divers, doctors, nurses, soldiers, and police officers. One man would lose his life trying to rescue the boys.

The dangerous and complex rescue involved trained divers navigating narrow underground passages filled with murky water and unpredictable currents in order to reach the boys and their coach and then bring them to safety. Once they found them, the boys had to be outfitted with diving gear and sedated so that they would not panic during the three-hour underwater journey back through the flooded passages to the cave entrance. They were tethered to the professional divers who had to navigate the narrow passages while protecting the boys. Amazingly, all were brought to safety.

There was no way those boys could escape that cave on their own. They needed someone to intervene, rescue them from the peril they faced, and bring them out. Someone who cared enough about them to step into their need. Someone who was able to pull off what seemed impossible.

Rescue is the first act of redemption.

The event in the Old Testament that defines redemption for the people of Israel is a rescue mission—the exodus, when God brought his people out of slavery in Egypt. It fits the basic structure of a redemption story perfectly. The people of God are enslaved, oppressed by a powerful and evil ruler who despises them. They are powerless to change their fate. Their captivity in Egypt mocks Israel's God and the promises he made to Abraham. What will God do to alleviate their suffering and show himself to be the one true God? He steps into their travail, rescues them from captivity, and ultimately restores them to the land he had promised.

Exodus 6:2–8 reveals God's heart in rescuing his people from their captivity in Egypt:

> God also said to Moses, "I am the LORD. I appeared to Abraham, to Isaac and to Jacob as God Almighty, but by my name the LORD I did not make myself fully known to them. I also established my covenant with them to give them the land of Canaan, where they resided as foreigners. Moreover, I have heard the groaning of the Israelites, whom the Egyptians are enslaving, and I have remembered my covenant.
>
> "Therefore, say to the Israelites, 'I am the LORD, and I will bring you out from under the yoke of the Egyptians. I will free you from being slaves to them, and I will redeem you with an outstretched arm and with mighty acts of judgment. I will take you as my own people, and I will be your God. Then you will know that I

> am the LORD your God, who brought you out
> from under the yoke of the Egyptians. And I will
> bring you to the land I swore with uplifted hand
> to give to Abraham, to Isaac and to Jacob. I will
> give it to you as a possession. I am the LORD.'"

Note the language of redemption in this passage: God responds to their suffering. He knows that they cannot escape on their own. He will bring them out, set them free, and redeem them because he alone is powerful enough to do it. He will restore them to a relationship with himself and the life he promised them. And he did just what he said he would do.

This powerful act of redemption becomes the defining event in how the people of Israel understand their God. "To know the Lord for who he is means knowing him as redeemer," observes biblical scholar W. Ross Blackburn. "Israel never knew the Lord as anyone other than the Lord her God who brought her out of Egypt. In other words, whatever else Israel may have known about God, she knew him firstly as her savior, and did not know him otherwise."[3]

Through this amazing rescue of his people from the oppressive rule of Pharaoh, God made himself known to his own people in a way they would remember and recount from that day forward. But he didn't redeem his people just so *they* would know their God. Remember, everything God does is to reveal himself to *all* peoples, including the Egyptians. And we see this clearly in the events of the exodus.

God makes it clear to Pharaoh that he is going to make himself known in ways never before seen or experienced. Through the plagues, God reveals to his people *and* to the Egyptians that he is more powerful than Pharaoh and Egypt's gods. But that's not all. The Lord tells Pharaoh that he is using him to make himself known in all the earth. After six devastating plagues, Pharaoh's heart remains hardened and he continues to resist. Then the Lord says to him, "For by now I could have stretched out my hand and struck you and your people with a plague that would have wiped you off the earth. But I have raised you up for this very purpose, that I might show you my power and *that my name might be proclaimed in all the earth*" (Exodus 9:15–16; emphasis added). And that's exactly what happens. As the people of Israel make their way toward the land God had promised them, the nations they encounter have already heard what their God has done to the Egyptians.

Although Pharaoh continually hardens his heart and rejects God, we see some Egyptians responding differently. After God warns them of the devastating effects of the hail that will fall on them, we read, "Those officials of Pharaoh who feared the word of the LORD hurried to bring their slaves and their livestock inside" (9:20). Later we see some of Pharaoh's officials acknowledge that God is too powerful and that "Egypt is ruined" (10:7). It's clear that some within Pharaoh's inner circle had come to believe that the God of Moses was more powerful than the gods of the Egyptians. When God works on behalf of his own people, he does it so that all people can see that he is more powerful than any other god.

And it happens just that way. When God's people are finally freed from Egypt, we read that "many other people" leave with them (12:38). Who were these people? They were most assuredly not the descendants of Abraham. This group likely includes other foreigners in Egypt and even some Egyptians who are choosing to follow the God who has shown he is more powerful than all the gods of Egypt. "If this is the case," Blackburn reasons, "then the plagues not only served as a means of judgment, but also as a means of mercy, that the Egyptians might come to know the Lord as God, and in so doing find refuge from the judgment that was to come upon the whole land."[4]

I've never been in a truly life-threatening situation where I needed someone to rescue me. But my family has. A few years ago, our son-in-law and two of our grandchildren were hit head-on by a drunk driver who crossed into their lane at over sixty miles an hour. His vehicle exploded on impact and burned. The driver died at the scene. Our son-in-law's mangled car also began to burn. Although suffering multiple injuries, he was able to get out of the burning car and pull his two-year-old daughter out of her car seat. Then his shattered right leg collapsed and he could not get to his son strapped into a car seat on the other side of the vehicle. In God's mercy, passersby stopped at the scene of the accident and rescued our four-year-old grandson from the car before it was too late. First responders arrived soon thereafter and provided the medical care needed to keep our son-in-law alive until they could airlift him and the four-year-old to two different emergency surgical centers. At their moment of greatest need, when all of their resources were exhausted, they were rescued. That rescue still brings tears to my eyes.

God rescues his people from certain death when there is nothing they can do to save themselves. Rescue is the first great act of redemption.

RESTORATION. "Christmas. December 25th, 1940." That's the inscription scrawled in pencil on the side of a drawer in an old piece of furniture my wife and I received from my maternal grandmother's house. It is a chifforobe, a closet substitute with drawers on one side and a wardrobe for hanging clothes on the other. This particular chifforobe has a pretty, etched mirror on the wardrobe door. It was painted pale green when we found it in her home after she went to be with the Lord at the ripe old age of ninety-seven.

Soon after bringing the chifforobe to our home, we started refinishing it. We stripped off three different coats of paint—

white, yellow, and that pale green. It was no easy task. After finally stripping the last coat of paint, we gently sanded the raw wood and treated it with Danish oil. As we worked in the oil, the color and grain of the wood emerged. What had been lost under three coats of enamel was brought out. The character and beauty of the wood were restored.

Restoration is the second great act of redemption, and we can see it as clearly in the exodus narrative as rescue. Rescue wasn't enough. It was one thing to be rescued from their oppressors in Egypt, but it was a whole other thing to find a new place to live, a place that they could call their own. God had promised to do that when he said to them, "And I will bring you to the land I swore with uplifted hand to give to Abraham, to Isaac and to Jacob. I will give it to you as a possession. I am the LORD" (Exodus 6:8). In other words, God promises to restore Abraham's descendants to the land that he gave their forefathers after he rescues them.

And that's exactly what he does. Although the path of restoration to their homeland had far more detours and took far longer than they desired, ultimately God brings them to the land he promised to Abraham, Isaac, and Jacob. All along the way, two things become evident: (1) God is more powerful than any of the nations that resist his plan to restore his people to the land, and (2) the temptation to worship other gods is too powerful for his people to resist.

After God's powerful rescue of his people from captivity in Egypt and the promise to restore them to their land, we would expect that they would remain faithful to him. But Israel's history is not that straightforward. Idolatry and rebellion rear their ugly heads even before the people make it to the Promised Land. And even though God miraculously goes before them as they take possession of it, the cancer of idolatry begins to grow again in Israel much sooner than one would expect. Most of the

Old Testament is the story of the struggle of God's people to remain faithful in the land where God restored them. They are "the redeemed," rescued from Egypt and restored to the land. But they choose not to live as the redeemed, faithfully obeying their Redeemer. Instead, they chase after false gods and abandon the one who rescued and restored them. The historical and prophetic books of the Old Testament tell the sordid tale of Israel's refusal to remain faithful to their God.

So what will God do with them now? How will he respond to their rebellion and wanton pursuit of other gods?

God responds to their rebellion just as he did when Adam and Eve sinned—with justice, mercy, and grace. He judges them harshly, punishes them for their idolatry, and ultimately causes them to be exiled from the land through its conquest by the kings of Assyria and Babylon. In his mercy, however, God does not abandon them completely. He promises that there will be a remnant who will return from exile to the land of promise. And in his grace, God rescues his people from exile and restores them to the land that he had promised. Once again, God redeems his people.

Putting It All Together

Reading the Bible as a redemption story helps me make sense of the Old Testament. I have to confess that I used to avoid reading it because it was just too hard to understand. The parts didn't seem to fit together in a way that made sense to me. Reading it as a redemption story, however, helps connect the dots. After the call of Abraham in Genesis 12, the exodus and the exile form the axles around which the history of God's people moves forward. They are the historical points of reference we can use to create a sense of cohesion and meaning for most of the Old Testament.

We humans need points of reference to bring a sense of order and meaning to what we see. My wife and I recently visited the

Denver Art Museum to explore an exhibition entitled Claude Monet: The Truth of Nature. The exhibition ended with a small collection of works from the more than 250 paintings that Monet composed in his private garden in Giverny, France. The most famous of these paintings are his *Water Lilies* series. Three paintings of the same scene, entitled *The Japanese Footbridge*, particularly captured our attention.[5] Each contains the same elements: a pond, water lilies, a bridge, and surrounding bushes and trees. Each was painted from the same perspective, looking over the water and the lilies to the bridge and beyond. Each explores one of Monet's fascinations: the effect of light and reflection on water. Each is stunningly beautiful. The second and third paintings are more impressionistic than the first, the shapes and objects less defined. But one thing remains the same: Monet uses the bridge as a point of reference in the center of each painting. It creates a sense of order and gives meaning to the whole. The colors, the technique, the composition—everything about those paintings creates a visual feast that touched us deeply. But we noticed that our attention kept returning to the bridge as we took in the beauty of the whole. It became the point of reference we needed to fully enjoy all the marvelous details of those masterpieces.

The exodus and the exile are the points of reference that give a sense of order to the widely varied literature of the Old Testament. They provide the structure we need to see how the story flows and develops from the call of Abraham in Genesis 12 to the end of the last book, Malachi. Both are redemption events.

How do the various parts fit together? In the books of the Law (Genesis through Deuteronomy), God reveals himself as the Redeemer and tells the redeemed how they should live. In the historical books (Joshua through Esther), we get a no-holds-barred look at how the redeemed failed to live out their identity as the redeemed, paid the price for their idolatry in the exile, and experienced redemption in their return to the land. In Job we are given a fascinating picture of the Redeemer's sovereignty and mercy while in the Song of Songs we see just how marvelous is his gift of love. In the Psalms, we are invited into the sometimes raw, sometimes inspiring worship of the Redeemer by his people, and in the wisdom literature (Proverbs and Ecclesiastes) we see how his wisdom ought to shape the way the redeemed live.

And then there are the prophetic books (Isaiah through Malachi). They provide a theological interpretation of the events that unfold in the historical books and a beautiful picture of the character of Israel's God. We might be tempted to see them as ancient news commentators. And to a degree that's okay. But they're much, much more than mere commentators. They are the voice of God. They speak God's commentary, his perspective, on what's happening and what will happen to his people and the surrounding nations.

And God doesn't pull any punches. Through the prophets, he rails against the idolatry of those whom he rescued from Egypt and restored to the land. He warns them of impending judgment and the destruction of Jerusalem. The description of what awaits those who refuse to worship him alone is not for the faint of heart. In chapter after chapter, God lays out his case against his rebellious people. Reading the prophetic books can be quite difficult, especially if we detach them from the two historical and theological reference points of exodus and exile.

But the prophetic books don't contain just descriptions of idolatry and God's judgment. Far from it. Sprinkled throughout long litanies of sin and its consequences, we find words of hope and images of restoration. Like the early summer wildflowers that push their way through the remaining snow cover in an alpine meadow, these verses hint at a future beauty that present realities still hide.

Through the words given to the prophets, God establishes a vision of a restored kingdom that transcends anything they have ever experienced. The earth will be filled with the knowledge of the Lord, he will dwell with his people, justice will be perfected, wars will cease, the law will be written on their hearts, and his Spirit will bring to life those who were spiritually dead (Habakkuk 2:14; Isaiah 2:3–5; 11:9; Jeremiah 31:33–34; Ezekiel 37:13). This vision of the future is replete with the language of redemption.

Most of these prophecies are given when God's people are facing the threat of exile or are already displaced from their homeland. Can you imagine the power of the promise and the vision of this restoration? Living in exile, God's people are tempted to despair, to doubt that God will rescue them from captivity and restore them to the land. And in their doubt, the foreign gods of Assyria, Babylon, and Persia seem ever more attractive. But God constantly reminds them of his power to redeem and their identity as his own (see Isaiah 43:1). He reassures them that their exile will come to an end, for he will redeem them once again and the whole world will hear what he has done (Isaiah 48:20). Notice how the news of this great redeeming act of God is to be proclaimed "to the ends of the earth." Everything God does is to make himself known to all peoples so that they too may worship him and find the fullness of life in him.

Restoration is always on God's mind. It is always his goal. The completion of God's redemption will be the establishment of his promised kingdom in which the tragic consequences of Adam's and Eve's rebellion—sin, death, and evil—are finally eliminated. That promise also gives us hope as we navigate a world that isn't yet all that God created it to be.

I bet that's a story my seatmate would have liked to hear.

6

REDEMPTION IN THE NEW TESTAMENT (CONSUMMATION)

All great redemption stories move toward a climactic encounter between good and evil. It's that moment when, against all odds, a hero defeats evil and rescues those who have been imperiled by it. It's the decisive battle in *Harry Potter and the Deathly Hallows* when Harry defeats the evil Lord Voldemort. It's the climax of *The Lion, the Witch and the Wardrobe* when Aslan rises from the dead, kills the White Witch, and sets her captives free.

The climactic event in a redemption story is like the neck of an hourglass, that narrow throat through which all of the sand flows from top to bottom. Everything above the neck flows toward it and then flows out of it. In a redemption story everything in the narrative moves toward this climactic victory, and the rest of the story then develops from it.

The Redeemer

The death of Jesus Christ on the cross is that climactic victory in the story of the Bible. On the cross Jesus defeats the universal enemies that no human has ever been able to overcome—sin, death, and evil. This is the decisive victory in the story of God's redemptive mission, the nexus from which everything in the Bible finds its point of reference. From its beginning, the story of the Bible flows toward the death of Christ. And once the victory is won, everything else in the story is grounded in that victory. His death is the neck of the hourglass where all the elements of the story coalesce and then move forward. His death accomplishes redemption.

Nothing could be clearer in Scripture than this: Jesus is the Redeemer. He is the perfect embodiment of God's desire that all people might know and worship him, the centerpiece of God's redemptive mission.

During the four hundred years between the events described at the end of the Old Testament and those we read about in the beginning of the New Testament, God's people yearn for redemption. They remember that God rescued and restored their ancestors from slavery in Egypt and from exile in Babylon. Surely, he would do it again. Their hope rests in the promise of a Messiah, one sent from God who would step into the lives of his people, rescue them from their oppressors, and restore them to the glorious kingdom promised to David and wondrously described by the prophets of old. By the time of Jesus's birth, their yearning for God to intervene on their behalf has not died away. In fact, it remains the all-encompassing hope of Israel.

I was recently on a flight with a soldier returning from his tour of duty in "an undisclosed location" in the Middle East. He couldn't wait to get home to his wife and three children. When he came out of the secured area of the airport, shrieks of joy, applause, homemade posters, balloons, hugs, kisses, and plenty of tears greeted him. Daddy was home. I imagine this moment was all his wife and kids thought about during those long months while they waited, prayed, and hoped they would see him again. The all-encompassing hope of his young family had been realized. Not just a few of us were wiping our eyes as we watched this joyous reunion.

The events surrounding Jesus's birth confirm that Israel's all-encompassing hope of redemption is being realized. An angel announces to Joseph in a dream that he and Mary should name their child Jesus, "because he will save his people from their sins" (Matthew 1:21). The language of "saving" in the New Testament refers to deliverance or rescue, the first great act of redemption. Jesus is the Redeemer, the one who will rescue his people from oppression. Mary, Joseph, Elizabeth, Zechariah, Simeon, and Anna all see it (see Matthew 1:18–24 and Luke 1:26–2:40). They are convinced that he is the one who will restore the promised kingdom. They believe their long-delayed hope has finally been realized. Redemption has come because the Messiah, the Redeemer, has been born.

There are a lot of different terms used in the New Testament to describe what Jesus accomplished on the cross: *forgiveness, justification, atonement, reconciliation, propitiation,* and others. I have to confess that it was difficult for me to bring them all together into some kind of clear and comprehensive understanding of what the death of Christ really means. Each illuminated an important part of what Jesus accomplished on the cross. But when I began to read the Bible as a story, it became clear to me that *redemption* summarizes the full scope of the work of Christ on the cross; it is the term that ties the story of the Bible together from beginning to end, and it grounds the death of Christ in God's great mission.

The language of redemption is found throughout the Gospels. For example, in Jesus's first public ministry he reads passages from the prophet Isaiah that foretold the redeeming work of the promised Messiah:

> Jesus returned to Galilee in the power of the Spirit, and news about him spread through the whole countryside. He was teaching in their synagogues, and everyone praised him.
>
> He went to Nazareth, where he had been brought up, and on the Sabbath day he went into the synagogue, as was his custom. He stood up to read, and the scroll of the prophet Isaiah was handed to him. Unrolling it, he found the place where it is written:
> "The Spirit of the Lord is on me,
>   because he has anointed me
>   to proclaim good news to the poor.
> He has sent me to proclaim freedom for
>   the prisoners
>   and recovery of sight for the blind,
> to set the oppressed free,
>   to proclaim the year of the Lord's favor."
>
> (Luke 4:14–19)

As Jesus comes back to the town where he had grown up, his reputation precedes him. On the way through Galilee, he has performed miracles and taught with an authority that no other teacher possessed. So, when he gets to his hometown, people expect him to perform among them the same kind of miracles they heard he had done in the other cities. After all, he is one of them.

He goes into the synagogue and, like any other Jewish male in good standing, is invited to read from the Hebrew Scriptures. He chooses two Old Testament passages, one from Isaiah 61:1–2 and the other from Isaiah 58:6. Both speak about the work of the long-hoped-for Messiah. Notice the language describing what Messiah will do when he comes—proclaim freedom, recovery, and liberation. Woven into Isaiah's prophetic vision of the one who comes in the name of the Lord is the language of redemption.

Jesus's very next words stun those who are present: "Today this scripture is fulfilled in your hearing" (Luke 4:21). He couldn't make it any clearer. The one who will rescue Israel and restore the kingdom is standing in their midst! They don't know how to respond. On the one hand, they want to believe that he is the promised Redeemer. If he is, they think, he will surely do even greater miracles in his hometown than they have heard he has done in other villages. On the other hand, they can't quite believe that this hometown boy, someone they've known since childhood, could be the Messiah.

Surprise and anticipation mixed with a dose of skepticism; those are powerful emotions. It's no wonder Jesus's childhood friends and neighbors try to kill him when he assures them that the Redeemer will rescue and restore believing Gentiles before he will bless his own unrepentant people (Luke 4:22–30).

The miracles and teachings of Jesus throughout his life model redemption His liberating, restoring, life-giving touch is available to all. He heals Jew and Gentile, men and women, young and old. When he casts out demons, he rescues people from suffering and restores them to life. And when he explains God's word and God's character in ways never heard before, he frees people from the Pharisees' onerous teachings and restores people to a relationship with their loving heavenly Father. Jesus's ministry throughout the land of Israel—healing, comforting, encouraging, and liberating—foreshadows the work of redemption he will accomplish on the cross.

Redemption Accomplished: The Cross

It all comes down to this: the crucifixion of Jesus Christ. Everything in the Bible before the cross points to it; everything in the Bible after the cross flows from it.

The apostle Paul embraces the centrality of the cross in his own life and ministry. He writes to the Corinthian church, "For I resolved to know nothing while I was with you except Jesus Christ and him crucified" (1 Corinthians 2:2). We know Paul talked about a lot of issues in his letters to the Corinthians. How then could Paul say that he resolved to know nothing while he was with them except "Jesus Christ and him crucified"? Martin Luther's famous dictum "The cross is the test of everything"[1] captures what Paul meant. Everything Paul said, wrote, and did found its point of reference in the crucifixion of Jesus Christ.

In her fine book *The Crucifixion: Understanding the Death of Jesus Christ*, Fleming Rutledge affirms the significance of the crucifixion. "Without the cross at the center of the Christian proclamation, the Jesus story can be treated as just another story about a charismatic spiritual figure." She adds, "It is the crucifixion that marks out Christianity as something definitively different in the history of religion. *It is in the crucifixion that the nature of God is truly revealed . . . the crucifixion is the most important historical event that has ever happened.*"[2]

Take a moment to digest what you've just read: "*The crucifixion is the most important historical event that has ever happened.*" That's a bold claim. It's also true. Without the cross there is no Christian faith. Without the cross there is no forgiveness of sins. Without the cross there is no redemption. We cannot know God truly apart from the cross.

That's why every person's identity is shaped in relationship to the cross, and every person's destiny is determined by their relationship to the cross. And that's why Paul can say there are ultimately only two kinds of people in the world—those for whom the cross is foolishness and those for whom it is the power of God for salvation (1 Corinthians 1:18).

A friend of ours was looking for some jewelry at one of the kiosks in a sprawling shopping mall. When she asked to see one of the crosses in the display case, the salesperson asked, "Do you mean one of these with the little man on it?"

Our friend asked, "Do you know who that person on the cross is?"

"No," he replied, "but he seems to be quite popular."

"His name is Jesus."

"Oh, I've heard of Jesus, but I didn't know that was him on the cross. I know some of his teachings like, 'Love your neighbor as yourself.' But why is he on these crosses?"

This conversation made me think back to the one on that flight out of Paris when my seatmate asked, "What's that book about?" If redemption accomplished through the death of Jesus Christ on the cross wasn't the centerpiece of my answer to his question, I missed the message of the Bible.

The Scope of Redemption

We humans take a lot of pride in being problem solvers. We tackle all kinds of problems—technical, mechanical, medical, relational, social, and many, many more. And we love stories about those who face imminent disaster and then figure out a way to fix the problem that caused it. I remember watching *Apollo 13*, a 1995 docudrama about the aborted lunar mission in 1970. An onboard explosion during the mission puts the three American astronauts in grave danger. Throughout the film the astronauts, mission controllers, and NASA engineers must creatively solve problem after problem in order to bring the three-man crew safely back to earth.

Can they do it? Can they resolve these issues in time to save the astronauts? Those are the questions the film makes us ask. As systems fail onboard, the tension mounts and tempers flare. Yet, step by agonizing step, they figure out how to get the crew back to earth safely. And when that space capsule splashes down and all three astronauts emerge alive, a thankful nation rejoices. What a powerful testimony to the human capacity to solve complex problems.

But the humbling truth is that we humans can't solve every problem. In fact, there are three universal problems that no mere mortal, no matter how ingenious or powerful, has ever been, or ever will be, able to solve—sin, death, and evil. As the Bible narrates it, these three destructive realities have bedeviled and punished humanity since the first humans rebelled. They still do. We all sin and bear its consequences. We all must submit to the inevitably of death. We all experience evil and rue its destructive power in our world. We might be able to mitigate their impact, but we cannot rid our lives of sin, death, and evil.

That's why we need a Redeemer, someone who can rescue us from these three unrelenting enemies and restore us to the life God created us to have. That's why God himself had to take action on our behalf. That's why it all comes down to the cross. Because he defeats sin on the cross, death cannot have the final word. And because the grave's deafening roar is silenced, evil will not have the final word. That's redemption accomplished.

For centuries Christians have used a threefold affirmation to declare the full scope of redemption. It goes like this: "Christ has died! Christ is risen! Christ will come again!"

CHRIST HAS DIED! Redemption could never be accomplished without resolution of our sin problem. And our sin problem could never be resolved until the penalty for it was paid. Everyone sins. The Bible is clear about that. Every book of the Bible demonstrates the scope and severity of our sin problem, sometimes in more graphic detail than we wish. The apostle Paul sums up this harsh reality with a bold assertion: "For all have sinned and fall short of the glory of God" (Romans 3:23). Because everyone sins, we all must pay the penalty of our sin. What is that penalty? Death. Paul says it this way in Romans 5:12: "Death came to all people, because all sinned."

Okay, I'll admit it. I've had a speeding ticket or two in my lifetime. And I deserved them. Each ticket cost me a pretty penny. The penalty for breaking the law was the payment of a fine. It had to be paid or the offence would stay on my record. The price for clearing my record was more than I thought it should be, but it had to be paid.

Compared to humanity's sin problem, a speeding ticket is trivial. But the requirement of paying a fine as the penalty for breaking the law works as an analogy for humanity's sin problem. The penalty has to be paid or the offense remains on our record. But that's not all. The penalty for sin has to be paid because God is just. He cannot ignore sin. His justice demands that the penalty for sin be paid. On the cross Jesus took on our sin and paid the price of our penalty. In the New Testament, the payment of that price is called a ransom.

In chapter 5 we explored two foundational acts of redemption—rescue and restoration. Ransom is the third act. Although ransom is introduced in the Old Testament,[3] this concept finds its fullest explanation in the New Testament. In Mark 10:45, we see Jesus using the language of ransom to describe why he was sent by the Father: "For even the Son of Man did not come to be served, but to serve, and to give his life as a ransom for many." We also see the use of a financial metaphor for ransom in 1 Corinthians 6:19–20 when Paul reminds his readers, "You are not your own; you were bought at a price."[4] But that's not all. Paul makes it clear that Jesus's death was a ransom for all people. He writes in 1 Timothy 2:5–6, "For there is one God and one mediator between God and mankind, the man Christ Jesus, who gave himself as a ransom for all people."

Let's not rush past that last paragraph. Jesus paid the penalty for everyone's sin. Mine. Yours. Everyone's. All of us deserve to die; none of us deserve this eye-popping, jaw-dropping, head-shaking, breathtaking act of redemption. That's what the Bible calls grace. The cross epitomizes God's grace.

We have to be careful not to think of Jesus's death on the cross only in terms of personal salvation and the forgiveness of our individual sins. It also has cosmic ramifications. Since his death on the cross secured ultimate victory over sin, death, and evil, he has unmatched authority over all earthly and heavenly powers (Matthew 28:18). That's why we have to see him as not only our Savior but also our King.

Most of the readers of this book likely live in the United States, a country founded through rebellion against a king. That makes it particularly difficult for us to imagine Jesus as king, much less embrace him as such. Plus, kings don't typically establish their reign through death and defeat. That normally happens through some kind of glorious military victory. From the world's perspective, Jesus's death on the cross is the ultimate defeat. How could he possibly be a king?

In order to make sense of the assertion that Jesus is our king, we have to see him in light of the promises God gave to his people in the Old Testament and the expectations of those who were waiting for these promises to be fulfilled. The prophets in the Old Testament had proclaimed that God would send the Messiah, the promised king who would establish a kingdom that no one could assail. This King, unlike all earthly kings, would rule with absolute justice. He would vanquish all those who oppose him and restore God's people to the land and the prosperity he had promised them. God's promises about what Messiah will do when he reigns make even the most outlandish campaign promises of our own politicians seem trivial. And unlike the promises we hear from candidates today, they are not based on wishful thinking or outright deception. The promises concerning the Messiah are as true as the very character of the One True God.

When Jesus was born, God's people had been waiting for this Messiah for centuries. They yearned for him to establish the promised kingdom, defeat all of Israel's enemies, and set all things right. But that possibility seemed far-fetched. They came face-to-face with Rome's power every day. They saw it in the magnificent structures Herod the Great erected throughout the land. They saw it in the presence of Roman soldiers in the cities and villages. And they felt it when they paid the taxes that the despised Romans demanded and extracted from those who worked every day to make ends meet. Roman power hung in the air; it seeped and crawled into every area of life in first-century Israel. And the people hated it. The seemingly unassailable power of Rome constantly reminded them that God hadn't done what he said he would do.

God's people yearned for the promised one who would rescue them from the political, economic, and military oppression of the Romans. They believed their redemption would come by the strength of a crusading Messiah, not the suffering of a crucified Savior. When we read the New Testament, we have to remember that this belief framed everything Jews thought about their God.

When some of the people see Jesus's miracles and hear his teaching, they call him "Messiah," and he does not deny it. He even claims that the kingdom is "here" (Mark 1:14–15). But when he does nothing to overthrow the Romans, it's almost like he's speaking nonsense. The one miracle they all longed to see— Romans running for their lives before a king whom they cannot stand up to—doesn't happen. No wonder most of the people in Israel during the time of Jesus simply cannot believe he is the Messiah.

I've heard Christians ask, "How could the Jews have missed Jesus?" I think the more relevant question is, "How could they have possibly seen Jesus as Messiah?" He met none of their expectations.

Nonetheless, no one had ever witnessed miracles like those Jesus did. And no one had ever heard anyone teach with such penetrating clarity and undeniable authority. In equal measure, the people Jesus encounters are intrigued and confused. Even some of those who follow him move from faith to doubt and back to faith fairly frequently. On the one hand, Jesus doesn't meet their expectations of Messiah. On the other hand, everything Jesus says and does tantalizes them with the possibility that he *might* be the Messiah.

We see this confusion in John the Baptist. John's ministry has been built on proclaiming Jesus as Messiah and calling people to repentance. When he is imprisoned by King Herod, John sends his disciples to Jesus to ask, in effect, "Are you the Messiah?" (see Matthew 11 and Luke 7). It seems clear that John asks this question honestly. The Romans are still in power and John is presently suffering at their hand. That's not the way John envisioned the coming of Messiah. When John's disciples come to Jesus, the phrasing they use could be translated, "Aren't you the Messiah? We thought you were!" To address their uncertainty, Jesus simply directs them to reflect on what they have seen and heard. "Go back and report to John what you have seen and heard: The blind receive sight, the lame walk, those who have leprosy are cleansed, the deaf hear, the dead are raised, and the good news is proclaimed to the poor" (Luke 7:22). The language Jesus uses comes from passages describing what will happen in the kingdom that Messiah will bring (see Isaiah 29:18–19; 35:5–6; and 61:1–2, for example).

For three years, Jesus's miracles confirm the coming of his kingdom and his teaching describes its nature. It's no wonder that as Jesus nears Jerusalem, "the people thought that the kingdom of God was going to appear at once" (Luke 19:11). They exult in his entry into Jerusalem because they believe that finally what they've yearned for will come true. Yet not that many days later, Jesus is hanging lifeless on a cross, a victim of the most dehumanizing form of execution ever devised. When that heavy stone rolls into place at the entrance to the tomb where they laid his lifeless body and the Roman soldiers take their place on either side of it, the dream that Jesus might be the Messiah shatters. Some king he turned out to be. It's no wonder his disillusioned followers hide, defeated, deflated, and afraid. It's hard to imagine the emotional whiplash they've experienced.

I'm not a big fan of roller coasters. You know what it's like. You sit in a cramped car and someone who looks too young to have a driver's license slams a bar down on your knees as a "safety precaution." That ought to be the first clue that this is not a good idea. The car starts on a slight downslope until it reaches the bottom of a huge incline. As the chain drags it ever upward, your heart rate increases and your breathing gets shallower. It's exciting and anxiety-inducing in equal measure. Then you reach the top of that first incline and peer at a descent so impossibly steep that there seems no way the car can stay on the track. The plunge into the abyss causes your bottom to rise off the seat just enough to cause real panic before you're jerked into a hairpin turn that almost throws you out of the car. You're disoriented and clinging to anything you can grab. You've gone from exhilaration to terror to despair in a very short period of time. I think that pretty well describes what the disciples went through emotionally the week Jesus died.

That Friday evening and throughout the day Saturday, the disciples could not possibly believe that the humiliating and dehumanizing death Jesus endured is, in fact, the victory of God. How could they believe that a dead man brutally murdered by a sinful, violent, and evil regime has defeated sin, death, and evil? All that he had said about the kingdom just sounds like "rabbi talk" now. In their minds, he hasn't defeated sin, death, and evil—sin, death, and evil have defeated him.

CHRIST IS RISEN! The resurrection changes everything. It proves that the death of Jesus was indeed the victory of God over sin, death, and evil. When death cannot hold him in the grave, he demonstrates that sin is defeated and that evil will not have the final word. The resurrection validates his identity as Messiah and the claim that redemption is accomplished. The resurrection of Jesus Christ is God's shout to the world, "Jesus is Lord and there is no other!"

I don't know about you, but it sure doesn't seem to me that sin, death, and evil have been defeated. In fact, it seems like their fury only grows and the suffering they cause only increases. News of unspeakable acts of violence, injustice, and oppression assails us almost daily. Like the disciples after Jesus's death, I sometimes struggle to believe that redemption has indeed been accomplished.

Recently, a friend asked me this penetrating and uncomfortable question: "Right now, Mark, what keeps you following Jesus?" Her query struck those deepest chords of doubt that most of us have, the ones we're afraid to voice. Am I a fool to believe in Jesus? Did he really accomplish what the Bible says he did? Is the big story of the Bible even true?

She persisted through my silence, "Mark, right now, what keeps you following Jesus?"

Instinctively, I answered, "The resurrection."

The resurrection is a high-stakes reality. It's like gravity. If gravity weren't true, everything about life on earth would be different. It's the same with the resurrection. If Christ isn't raised from the dead, everything about our faith and lives would be empty. Paul makes it clear that if Jesus isn't raised from the dead, the gospel we preach is impotent, our faith is useless, we are liars about God, and we are the most pitiable people on the face of the earth (1 Corinthians 15:14–19). That's why the resurrection is, indeed, a high-stakes reality.

And Paul knows what he's talking about when he writes about the resurrection. He encountered the risen Christ on the road to Damascus and ended up blind, face-down in the dust. Through that experience, his whole life changes. Now he knows that the resurrection confirms everything Jesus said about the coming of the kingdom. He knows that because sin, death, and evil are defeated, those who believe in Jesus will be raised from the dead when he returns, and those who are alive on that day will be transformed (1 Corinthians 15:20, 51–57).

We believe that will happen. But it hasn't happened yet. So we wait for the final act in God's redemptive work and mission.

We have three children. Although each of my wife's pregnancies was somewhat different from the others, they all followed the same basic pattern: excitement followed by waiting followed by yearning for the baby to be born. A little anxiety kept crowding into the experience as well. Toward the end of each pregnancy, we couldn't wait to meet our new son or daughter. And I'm pretty sure my wife couldn't wait for the physical discomfort of a full-term pregnancy to be over. Waiting for the whole process to come to its completion, yearning to hold in our arms one who would change our lives, ready for the pain and discomfort to be over, the anticipation grew each day. And when we held each of those babies, all of that waiting, all of that discomfort, and all of the pain and trauma of childbirth was worth it.[5] And so is waiting for our redemption to be consummated.

CHRIST WILL COME AGAIN! Like all good tales, the story of the Bible moves toward a conclusion that ties together its themes, subplots, characters, and intrigues. The last act is the anticipated completion of a saga that began at the dawn of time, traverses the ages, frames the present, and gives hope for the future. Although we have to struggle at times to keep the arc and progress of the narrative in view as we read the Bible, the story is always there, always moving to its glorious end.

Have you ever seen a satellite image of the Mississippi River? Take just one stretch of this mighty river, the western boundary of the state of Mississippi, for example, and look at its path. To say that it's "curvy" would be an understatement. "Serpentine" doesn't even do it justice. The river's channel winds back and forth with seemingly little sense of pattern. Oxbow lakes along the way remind us that, in the past, the river had even sharper, more pronounced curves in some places than we can see today. Yet, the river is always moving toward the Gulf of Mexico. Always.

The story of the Bible is always moving toward its certain, inevitable, inescapable, foreshadowed, and glorious God-ordained end. Always.

And what is that end? The return of Jesus Christ, the consummation of God's redemptive mission, the blessed hope of the believer (Titus 2:13).

In the last two chapters of the Bible, Revelation 21 and 22, the apostle John sees a new heaven and a new earth. In the new heaven and the new earth, everything that was lost, damaged, and compromised through the rebellion of Adam and Eve is restored. Although the creation we experience today has many good, even magnificent features and experiences, we all carry this sense that life in this world isn't all that it was created to be. For those of us who know that human history is always moving toward the end God has ordained, we live with an essential "not-yet-ness" to our faith. We long for an "even more" kind of world, a world where the good things of life are even better.[6] The big story of the Bible takes us to the ending that we all long for when everything that's wrong in the world will be made right, everything that's broken in the world will be made whole, and everything that's ugly in the world will be made beautiful.

John's vision of a new heaven and a new earth is stunning. Everything is new (Revelation 21:5)! The very presence of God is the source of light and life as he dwells among his people (21:22–23; 22:5). In this new reality, people worship him with wholehearted devotion, free from the temptation to believe that there is more to life than what they currently have in his presence. No more sorrow! No more death! No more weeping! No more pain! All of this is true because Christ defeated sin, death, and evil on the cross (21:3–4). Unlike Eden where the serpent also dwelt, in the new heaven and the new earth there will be nothing impure, shameful, or deceitful, and no possibility of temptation and sin (v. 27). And, in the new heaven and the new earth, God's desire to be known and worshiped by all will be realized. His redemptive mission will be complete. People from every tongue, nation, tribe, and language will bring their tribute to him and experience his life-giving presence (v. 24). Oh, how we long for that day when redemption is perfected!

In *The Last Battle*, the finale of C. S. Lewis's Chronicles of Narnia, one of the characters describes the new Narnia that Aslan has beckoned his followers to enter and enjoy because he has defeated the witch. The Unicorn says, "I have come home at last! This is my real country! I belong here. This is the land I have been looking for all my life, though I never knew it till now. The reason why we love the old Narnia is that it sometimes looked a little like this. Bree-hee-hee! Come further up, come further in!"[7]

Between the Times

We live between the times. We live in the story of the Bible while we await its conclusion. On the one hand, we look back to the death and resurrection of Jesus Christ, thanking God for the redemption he accomplished. Yet on the other hand, we look forward to his promised return and to the ultimate completion, the consummation, of redemption. We are redeemed and yet we await redemption in its fulness. Our current experience of God's magnificent act of redemption in Christ—life eternal, forgiveness of sins, reconciliation with God, his daily presence in the person of the Holy Spirit, healing, freedom, peace, and much, much more—is just a taste, an aroma, a glimpse, a whisper of the consummation yet to come.

God's people are that taste, aroma, glimpse, and whisper of redemption the world longs for. We, the redeemed, are those through whom the Redeemer makes himself known. We, the people of his redemptive mission, are the down payment on the final act of redemption.

We'll explore that startling reality and privilege in the fifth and final thread woven throughout the big story of the Bible, the people of God.

PART THREE

CHARACTERS

Great stories have great characters. Or maybe we should say great characters make good stories great. Characters humanize stories. We identify with them and connect with them. They make us cry and laugh. They give us hope, inspire us, and make us angry. We fall in love with them and we fear them. As any good editor would remind us, "No story would be a story without characters to define it."[1]

God is the main character of the Bible. It's his story. But God isn't the sole actor in his story. He works through his people, the people of his redemptive mission, to drive the story forward and bring it to completion. The Bible has many great characters, unforgettable characters. Through them we find *ourselves* in the story, and that's when the story changes our lives.

CHAPTER

7

CHOSEN

When our family lived in Poland, we didn't know what to call ourselves. The labels we had used in the United States didn't work. If we called ourselves "Christian," most people thought we were Roman Catholic. If we called ourselves "evangelical," that meant we were Lutherans. "Baptist" didn't work because most Poles had never met or even heard of a Baptist.[1] Yet we had to call ourselves something. Many of our friends simply called themselves "believers," and that's what we chose.

What language do you use to describe yourself when it comes to your faith? To select just a few choices from the denominational buffet, you might say Baptist, Methodist, Presbyterian, or Pentecostal. Or you might think more broadly and call yourself Protestant or Roman Catholic. Some of us call ourselves Christian or, like our Polish friends, simply "believers." There's nothing wrong with any of these labels, but they definitely don't tell the whole story.

When we read the Bible as the story of God's redemptive mission, we discover another, more powerful and poignant way to think about ourselves. We are the people of God's mission.

One of the most surprising developments in the story of the Bible is that God chooses to accomplish his mission through his people. Scripture never tells us why God chooses to use humans as his agents to rule over creation. In the same way, it never tells us why God delegates the execution of his redemptive mission to us. But he does, and most of the text of the Bible describes how he creates, shapes, directs, instructs, corrects, protects, blesses, and judges his people so that they can live out their identity as the people of his mission.

We Are Part of God's Big Story

We are the people of God's mission. It is our very identity, not just one of the many things we might choose to do as believers. We live out that identity everywhere, every day, and in everything we do. Unfortunately, many Christians I've known through the years are unaware that's who we are. Why? When we don't read the Bible as the story of God's redemptive mission, we don't see ourselves as the people of that mission. In other words, we don't see ourselves in the story, and we don't connect to it at the deepest level.

Sometimes we muddy the way we think of our identity by throwing the word "calling" into the mix. For example, we say that some Christians are called to missions. Or we might say that someone is called to preach. Those two uses of "calling" betray a misunderstanding. The first has to do with geography and the latter focuses on what a person does. Calling, however, primarily relates to who we are, not to what we do or where we do it.

We need to change the way we use the language of calling to make sure it lines up with the way the Bible describes our calling. The Bible speaks consistently of believers as those who are called to be like Christ, called to salvation, and called out of the kingdom of darkness into the kingdom of his marvelous light. We're called to hope, to grace, to holiness, and to liberty. These concepts describe who we are more than what we're supposed to do or where we're supposed to go.[2]

Another misunderstanding emerges when we think of our identity and calling individualistically. We tend to get hung up on whether God has called us individually to a particular place or ministry. But what if we changed our approach and thought of both our identity and calling collectively. Our calling comes as a part of our identity as the people of God. We, as a community, are called to be the people of his mission. As a community, we are given a commission, a mandate, to make our Redeemer known to all peoples so that they may find the fullness of life in him.

Let's go back to that point in the story when God chooses the man through whom he creates the people of his mission.

God's Chosen People

You remember how the story unfolds in the early chapters of Genesis. Although God creates humans to live in perfect harmony with him and to enjoy life to the fullest, they rebel. In the face of that rebellion, God responds with justice, mercy, and grace. The first ten chapters of Genesis make one thing painfully clear: humanity is a mess, but God will not give up on us.

Near the end of Genesis 11, a new character steps into the story—Abraham,[3] son of Terah. His introduction into the narrative is rather unremarkable. Dozens of other names have appeared in the pages of the Bible up to this point, especially in Genesis 10. Most of them seem like placeholders that just serve to demonstrate population growth and the diversity of humanity. But don't be fooled by Abraham's casual introduction into the story. He is definitely not just a placeholder.

After recounting a long, post-flood list of ancestors, the narrative then narrows its focus and informs us, "This is the account of

Terah's family line. Terah became the father of Abraham, Nahor and Haran. And Haran became the father of Lot" (Genesis 11:27). We don't know much about Terah, Abraham's father, except that he is a descendant of Shem, the son Noah chose to bless above his two other sons. We also learn that Terah comes from Ur of the Chaldeans, a city located in what is now Iraq. Later in the Bible, we learn that Terah worshiped the gods of his homeland (Joshua 24:2).

You read that right. Abraham's father worshiped false gods, and it's a sure bet that Abraham worshiped the gods of his father too. Based on where they lived, we can assume Terah and his family were polytheists who worshiped gods representing the sun, stars, and the moon, as well as other gods associated with physical and spirit worlds.[4] Even though we know a little bit about Abraham's family and homeland, at this point we have no reason to think this man will be the key player in another major pivot in the story of the Bible. But he is.

> The LORD had said to Abram, "Go from
> your country, your people and your father's
> household to the land I will show you.
> > "I will make you into a great nation,
> >   and I will bless you;
> > I will make your name great,
> >   and you will be a blessing.
> > I will bless those who bless you,
> >   and whoever curses you I will curse;
> > and all peoples on earth
> >   will be blessed through you."
> >   (Genesis 12:1–3)

From this point forward, the trajectory of the story changes. God's call of Abraham to be the one through whom he will create his chosen people becomes a point of reference for every-thing that comes after it in the narrative.[5] That's why we can say with confidence that it is one of the most important events in biblical history. And yet, we know so little about it.

Scripture never really tells us why God chose Abraham out of the teeming masses of people described in Genesis 10 to become the progenitor of his people.[6] What we can see quite clearly, however, is that the narrative's focus now tightens from a picture of the greatly diverse human family to one man's family.

And we don't know how God communicated with Abraham. For all we know, Abraham could have been offering sacrifices to the false gods his family worshiped in Ur when the one true God interrupted and somehow spoke to him. Maybe God spoke in a mighty wind or revealed himself in an asteroid shower. Maybe in a still small voice or a vision. Isn't it interesting that the Bible doesn't even suggest an answer to this question?

Have you ever noticed how much white space there is on each page of the Bible? Between the letters, the words, the lines, and in the margins, that white space helps make the Bible readable. I like to think of the white space on a page as the place where all the questions we can't answer about biblical events and charac-ters reside. I sometimes like to venture into that white space and speculate about questions the text doesn't really answer. There's nothing wrong with that, by the way. It often humanizes the sto-ries. It also humbles me and makes me even more eager to read the rest of the text. And that's good.

I suspect that if the Bible told us how God revealed himself to Abraham, we might expect God to reveal himself to everyone that way. And then we might not hear God speaking to us, if he doesn't do it the way he spoke to Abraham. Or, if we knew why God chose him, maybe we would be tempted to venerate Abra-ham and conclude that he deserved God's favor.

We want to be like our heroes. As a little boy I wanted to be faster than a speeding bullet, more powerful than a locomotive, and able to leap tall buildings in a single bound. That's what Superman could do and he was my hero. He dwelled in my imagination day and night. I wanted to be just like Superman.

Maybe that's why the Bible doesn't answer our questions about God's encounter with Abraham. We need to be reminded that Abraham isn't the hero of this story. God is. Although we do well to learn from the lives of the Bible's amazing cast of characters, none of them, including Abraham, is perfect. Anyone who's read the Bible knows that for a fact. God is the one we should idolize and seek to imitate.

God's call of Abraham is pretty straightforward. "Go!" is not a suggestion for him to consider; it is a directive to be followed. The Hebrew text allows us to read it with intensity and urgency. Something like, "Get yourself up and get out of here!"[7]

It is no small matter for Abraham to obey this command. Fundamentally, everything that defines him and his future—his identity, security, and prosperity—God is telling him to leave. And not only that, God commands Abraham to leave without telling him where he should go. In essence, the command is, "Leave everything, and entrust your future to me. Leave your land, your people, your culture, the way of life you've known from childhood. Leave your past and step into a future that lies beyond your sight. Trust me, Abraham, and I will show you where to go."[8] That's not asking too much is it? Of course it is!

It would have been easy for Abraham to dig in his heels and question God's sanity for commanding him to go on this suicide mission. Yet, Genesis 12:4 says, "So Abraham went, as the LORD had told him." He leaves everything and obeys the voice of God. I suspect those who knew him were questioning Abraham's sanity when he pulled up stakes and left. He simply trusts and obeys God. As the old hymn puts it, "Trust and obey, for there's no other way"[9] to fully experience the goodness of God.

Abraham's decision to trust and obey God, even when doing so seemed crazy, has played a big part in our family's life. In the spring of 1988, we packed up our young children, and everything else we could fit into our Mitsubishi van, and left Austria to move to Poland. Unlike Abraham, at least we knew where we were going. Like Abraham, we went out of obedience, trusting God to provide. At that time a Communist government still ruled Poland and the USSR dominated the country politically, economically, and militarily. We went to Poland not really knowing what it might mean to live under a Communist regime. Some people questioned our sanity. I remember my uncle's response when I told him we were moving our young family to a Communist country: "You're a fool." I wouldn't be surprised to find out one day that Abraham had a relative who said something like that as well.

God's Promises

In between God's call in verse 1 and Abraham's response in verse 4, the Lord makes some very significant promises to him: "I will make you into a great nation, and I will bless you; I will make your name great" (Genesis 12:2). These promises form the basis of God's relationship with his people. It is a covenant relationship, one in which two parties make a binding agreement with one another.[10] The promises describe what God commits himself to do on Abraham's behalf. In order to experience the fulfillment of these promises, Abraham has to commit to leave everything and trust God to do what he has bound himself to do. Each of these promises packs a powerful punch and smacks of a future that Abraham could never have imagined.

"I WILL MAKE YOU INTO A GREAT NATION." What does it take to make a nation? Land with borders and a government of some sort would be the most commonly cited requirements. God's first promise implies that Abraham's descendants will have a distinct geographical and national identity. At this point Abraham has neither. In fact, he won't throughout his entire life. He lives as a nomad of sorts, a landless wanderer.[11]

God could have promised Abraham, "I will make you into a great family," or "I will make you into a great clan." But he doesn't. The promise is to make Abraham's descendants into a great nation. Nations are not defined by bloodlines. People from different families, clans, and tribes, and even ethnicities, can make up a nation. Although Abraham's family will be the foundation of the promised nation, the nation will include other families, clans, and peoples. Becoming a nation is a work Abraham can't do. It is the work that God promises to do. Abraham's obligation is to trust God and obey him.

"**I WILL BLESS YOU.**" Not only does God promise that a great nation will develop from Abraham's descendants, he also promises to prosper Abraham. Blessing in the Old Testament often implies material provision, even abundance. And God does this for Abraham. Boy, does he ever! In fact, Abraham and his son Isaac become so wealthy, the kings and rulers of the territories where they settle feel threatened by their presence (see Genesis 26:16). In the ancient world, wealth was measured by the number of family members, herds, servants, and possessions you had. In other words, a person's wealth was there for all to see; no hidden offshore accounts. Wealth created social and economic power. It also demonstrated the power of your gods. It's no wonder those who ruled over a particular region felt threatened by the presence of this wanderer who possessed such vast material wealth. It was clear to them that this man worshiped a powerful God.

"**I WILL MAKE YOUR NAME GREAT.**" In Abraham's time and cultural setting, a praiseworthy name was more treasured than herds, fields, servants, children, and gold. No material possession rivaled its value. God promises Abraham that he will enjoy a good reputation and be honored by others. Whereas abundant wealth means power, a great name means great influence. When God says, "I will make your name great," he's basically promising that others will speak well of Abraham and consider him as someone to be reckoned with, someone others had better listen to, someone whose God was worth knowing and worshiping.

It's clear that this third promise flows from the first two. If God makes a powerful and prosperous nation from Abraham's descendants, Abraham's reputation will be great indeed. And Abraham's God will have even greater renown.[12] When Abraham thrives and increases in number, those who know him will assume that his God is the reason for that blessing. And they will likely seek the blessing of Abraham's God because of his prosperity and reputation. In this way, God's desire to be known and worshiped by all will be realized through his people. That's a new paradigm for the way God will accomplish his mission. And it will dominate the rest of the big story of the Bible.

Although it's difficult to detect in most English translations, the next line in God's promises to Abraham differs somewhat from the previous ones. "And you will be a blessing" in Hebrew is actually God's follow-up command to, "Get yourself up and go!" Literally it says, "Be a blessing."

Hang in there with me for a couple of sentences while I nerd-out with some of the details of the Hebrew text. I want us to see that there's more to this phrase than we can typically see in our English translations. When there are two commands in a Hebrew text like this one, the second command often communicates the result or purpose of the first. That happens in English as well. For example, if I said to my son, "Go upstairs and clean up your room," I've given him two commands. "Go upstairs" and "clean up your room." He can obey the second command only if the first one is already done. "Clean up your room" is the real reason why I've told him to go upstairs. It's the purpose of his going upstairs.[13] So when we apply this understanding to Genesis 12:2, we see that God commands Abraham to leave his homeland so that he will become a source of blessing to others.[14] The purpose of God's blessing on Abraham's descendants is to create blessing for all of those among whom they will live.

Let's summarize God's interaction with Abraham up to this point. "Leave everything you know and love, even though I haven't told you where you're going. I can promise you this, I'm going to give you a lot of descendants, a lot of wealth, and a lot of honor in the eyes of others. And it's not just for your sake that I'm going to do all this; it's also for the sake of others."

I have to confess that for much of my Christian life, I didn't think of God's blessing this way. I was quick to thank the Lord for all that he had done for me. But I never thought of it in light of other people. I thought what he had done for me was just for me, for my benefit alone. When I began to read the Bible as the story of God's redemptive mission, however, I began to see that from the very beginning whatever God does for us is never just for our sake. It's always also for the sake of others. As the people of God, we are called to be mindful of how we can be a blessing to others as a living testimony to the greatness of our God. That changes how I think about my relationship with God. It brings my neighbors, coworkers, relatives, and the strangers I meet on a daily basis into that relationship. If I think about God's blessing in my life apart from his reason for blessing me, I've missed the point.

God isn't finished with Abraham yet. What comes next is even more spectacular.

"I WILL BLESS THOSE WHO BLESS YOU, AND WHOEVER CURSES YOU I WILL CURSE." Who is God going to bless through Abraham? God promises that he will seek the good of those who seek Abraham's good. In like manner, God promises to act against those who speak ill of Abraham and seek to do him harm.[15] When people get involved with Abraham they get involved with Abraham's God. They will come to know him as either the one who blesses or the one who curses. That depends on how they relate to God's chosen people.

In many ways, this promise acts as a protection for Abraham. God's intent is to bless others through Abraham, but in order to accomplish that, he may have to act against those who seek to harm or even destroy his people. When God's people are threatened with destruction, God's desire for all people to know and worship him is also threatened. That's why he will judge and act against those who oppose his mission by threatening the very existence of his people.

"AND ALL PEOPLES ON EARTH WILL BE BLESSED THROUGH YOU." But God still isn't finished with Abraham. The full scope of God's promises comes into view in the next line: "And all peoples on earth will be blessed through you." The promise of God's blessing extends to all the peoples of the earth. Everything God has just said to Abraham leads to this last line. It reveals the ultimate purpose of the two commands "go" and "be a blessing."

From the beginning of the big story of the Bible, we've seen that God's intent is universal. He desires that all worship him and find the fullness of life in him. Rather than just a personal promise to one man, through Abraham, God creates the pathway for all peoples to be blessed. New Testament scholar N. T. Wright says, "'Blessedness'. . . is what happens when the creator God is at work both *in* someone's life and *through* that person's life."[16] People come to know God through God's people. Yes, people can see something of God in creation and, yes, there are times when God reveals himself in visions and dreams, but the story of the Bible narrates how God makes himself known to *all* peoples through *his* people.

I didn't always see this critical truth. Early in my Christian journey, it seemed to me that God's sole concern in the Old Testament was Israel, the nation formed from Abraham's descendants. All of the other nations were portrayed as Israel's enemies, and it seemed like God turned toward Gentiles only after his people rejected their Redeemer, Jesus. But when I began to read the Bible as a story, it became clear that the Bible is the story of God's redemptive mission for *all people*. God's concern has always been for all people. And it always will be.

That's why God's promise to extend his blessing to all people is repeated throughout the Bible.[17] The apostle Paul picks up on the importance of this promise to Abraham. He writes,

> Understand, then, that those who have faith
> are children of Abraham. Scripture foresaw
> that God would justify the Gentiles by faith, and
> announced the gospel in advance to Abraham:
> "All nations will be blessed through you."
> (Galatians 3:7–8)

Notice that when Paul quotes the last line of Genesis 12:3, "all nations will be blessed through you," he calls this promise "the gospel announced beforehand."[18] Paul emphasizes that anyone who responds to the gospel by faith, regardless of whether they are Abraham's descendant or not, will be blessed. Paul's emphasis is consistent with the intent and scope of Genesis 12:3. Anyone, whether a descendant of Abraham or not, who by faith worships the God of Abraham will be blessed.[19] And not only that, when anyone believes in the God of Abraham, they become a part of God's chosen people.

We need to pause for a moment, step back from the details we've been working on, and see them in the light of the big story of the Bible. There's no doubt Genesis 12:1–3 is a pivot point in the story. Two big ideas emerge and are woven into the fabric of the story from here on out. First, God chooses one people through whom he will bless all peoples. Second, anyone who believes in Abraham's God becomes a part of God's chosen people. Just as Adam's and Eve's rebellion changed everything about humanity's relationship with God, so the creation of one special people changes the way God relates to humanity. He will fulfill his desire to be known and worshiped by all peoples through his chosen people.[20]

But the question remains, "How does God accomplish his redemptive mission through his people?" First and foremost, God does this through *the Redeemer*, Jesus. Descended from Abraham, Jesus is clearly and fully human. He accomplishes redemption on the cross and will bring it to completion when he comes again. Second, God fulfills his mission through *the redeemed*, those who have experienced God's redemption and are now privileged to live in ways that reveal him to all peoples. The mission of God is executed by the people of God; the Redeemer is revealed through the redeemed.

For five generations, my father's family put down deep roots in Putnam County, West Virginia. We lived in a small town with one stop light, one bank, and two grocery stores. It was a safe and comfortable place. We knew just about everyone in our little community, and they were all pretty much just like us. I used to jokingly say that the closest thing we had to an ethnic group in my hometown were the Episcopalians, and the only international food we had were French fries and Vienna sausages.

This whole idea of being part of a people chosen by God to live out his redemptive mission for all peoples never crossed my mind as a kid. It wasn't until I saw God use me in the lives of those who were very different from me that I began to imagine a life framed by that identity. My wife and I have lived into that imagination and seen the stunning diversity of the redeemed.

We've worshiped with God's people in a dirt-floored tent in Soweto, South Africa; a soaring sanctuary in Seoul, Korea; and an open stadium in Colombo, Sri Lanka. We've gathered in public and in secret, with thousands and with a few. We've heard hearts abandoned to their Redeemer, praising him in languages we do not know. And what we've experienced is but a tiny part of the redeemed people of God. The fulfillment of God's promise that all peoples would be blessed through Abraham is being spectacularly fulfilled.

8

UNIQUE

For more than the three decades, Fred Rogers shaped the hearts and minds of America's children through his daily television show, *Mister Rogers' Neighborhood*. An ordained Presbyterian minister and child development specialist, Rogers believed children need voices of security and affirmation to nurture their social and emotional growth. He spoke directly and genuinely to the children who watched, choosing to be himself rather than portraying a fictional character. Although his tone and message were positive and encouraging, Rogers wasn't afraid to tackle the tough issues children sometimes face like the death of a pet, sibling rivalry, going to a new school, and even divorce.

Mister Rogers spent a lot of time at the Youngs' house. Our kids loved his gentle presence, corny friends, hand puppets, and the adventures in the "Neighborhood of Make-Believe." Do you remember his song that began with the line, "You are my friend, you are special"? I wouldn't be surprised if you can hear the melody as you read those lyrics. And I bet you also remember him singing the line, "You are the only one like you." Our kids and millions of others believed Mister Rogers when he sang those lines. It's no wonder his show was aired for years.

"You are special." "You are the only one like you." Those are powerful and formative words. They help shape a clear and confident sense of self. Children need to believe them. Adults want to believe them.

Throughout the Old Testament God communicates those same messages to his chosen people. They are special. God chose them out of all the other nations. They are unique. Their God is unlike any other god and, as a result, they are to be unlike any other people. The same holds true for us today. But what does it mean for the people of God to be unique? How can we live out our special identity and calling to be the people of God's mission? To answer these questions, we need to go back to another critical event in the Old Testament. Like God's call of Abraham, this one also occurs outside the land of Canaan. On a mountain in the desert wilderness of Sinai, God gives his people the charter upon which he will build a unique nation.

The Founding of the Nation

No doubt about it, the promises God made to Abraham were game changers. They laid out a future that no one saw coming. A people formed from the descendants of one family would become the means through which God would make himself known to all peoples. From the time of the patriarchs (the stories of Abraham, Isaac, and Jacob in the book of Genesis) through the exodus from Egypt, the people of God were known as the children of Abraham. But God had promised that he would make Abraham's descendants into a blessed and renowned nation. Nations differ from clans and tribes in that the latter find their identity in a common ancestor. In contrast, nations have many family bloodlines and ethnicities, along with borders, laws, and governments that define, codify, and organize their way of life.

Exodus 19–20 describes the founding of the nation of Israel. When the children of Abraham receive the Ten Commandments directly from the hand of God, they receive the foundation, the charter they need to become a nation. This is a critical moment in the history of God's people, another pivot point in the big story of the Bible.

We have parallels in our own history. We celebrate the historical events and documents upon which our nation was founded. On July 4 each year we celebrate the Declaration of Independence, the document stating the rights and principles upon which a new independent nation would be founded. However, the adoption of the Declaration of Independence by the Second Continental Congress in 1776 did not create the governmental or legal structure for the new nation. That task remained unfinished until the ratification of the Constitution of the United States of America on June 21, 1788. The Constitution is the supreme law of the nation, the charter that sets forth the structure and functions of the federal government. It codifies the rights and principles set forth in the Declaration of Independence and establishes the legal precedent for all subsequent laws. Ultimately, every aspect of our lives as citizens of the United States of America is framed by the Constitution.

In many regards, Exodus 19–20 contains the Declaration of Independence and the Constitution for the nation God is forming out of Abraham's descendants. That's why these two chapters are so critical. They form the foundation for Israel's identity and way of life. But before we get into the details of this grand event, we need to stop and remind ourselves that, although something new is emerging in God's plan for his people, the purpose for which God is forming the nation of Israel remains the same as his purpose in choosing one family to be his own: so that all peoples, not just the children of Abraham, may know and be blessed by him. Never forget that. Never.

Israel's Identity

Just as the Declaration of Independence stated the "self-evident" truths that would define our nation's identity, Exodus 19:4–6 lays out the truths upon which the nation of Israel would build its identity. These are God's words to his people. They contain what he wants them to know about themselves. Before he tells them how they are to live, he tells them how they are to think about themselves. If we don't think of ourselves properly, we cannot be whom we are created to be and do what we are called to do. For example, we cannot live out our redemption until we adopt the story of redemption as our own. We cannot show the world the God we serve and love unless we've embraced our identity as his special people.

Here's how the Lord wants his people to think about themselves as he prepares to make them into a nation.

> "You yourselves have seen what I did to Egypt,
> and how I carried you on eagles' wings and
> brought you to myself. Now if you obey me fully
> and keep my covenant, then out of all nations
> you will be my treasured possession. [Because][1]
> the whole earth is mine, you will be for me a
> kingdom of priests and a holy nation." These
> are the words you are to speak to the Israelites.

REDEEMED. To give his people a deep sense of how their history shapes their identity, God first reminds them that he redeemed them from Egypt. This reminder reinforces in their minds that he is the one true God against whom no other nation and its gods can stand. The people had seen their God defeat the most powerful nation the world had ever seen and humiliate its gods in the process. Imagine the memories that these words would stir in the minds of the people. They remember the devastation of the plagues and the wails of despair as Egypt's parents lost every one of their firstborn sons. They remember the special Passover meal and the blood smeared on their doorframes so that the Lord would pass over their homes as he brought judgment on Egypt and her gods. In their memories, they could still hear the thunder of Pharaoh's chariots bearing down upon them at the edge of the Red Sea. And they remember God's miraculous parting of the waters and their trek on dry ground through a canyon with walls of raging water. God did all of this to rescue them from Egypt. Like the majestic eagle that carries its young on its back, God carried his people out of slavery (Deuteronomy 32:10–12). Their first point of identity is clear: they are the redeemed.

Although their redemption from Egypt was solely on the basis of God's mercy and grace, their enjoyment of the blessings of being the redeemed is conditioned on their obedience to him. God will lay out a way of life for them in the Law that will make them unique among the surrounding nations and ensure that they can prosper. But they must obey his Law and remain faithful to him in order to experience the fullness of his promised blessing. God is establishing another covenant relationship with his people. Biblical scholars call this second major binding agreement between God and his people the Mosaic covenant. Throughout the Old Testament, Israel is referred to as God's covenant people.

"MY TREASURED POSSESSION." How else does God want his people to think of themselves? They are, he reminds them, his treasured possession. Throughout the ages, kings and queens around the world have possessed special items that mean more to them than all the rest of their vast treasures and possessions. These treasured possessions point to the majesty, the power, the magnificence of those who possess them.

I still remember the first time we saw the Crown Jewels of the United Kingdom housed in the Tower of London, a stunning collection of 140 ceremonial objects used at the coronations of Britain's kings and queens. The precious gemstones in these objects include the largest clear cut diamond in the world, named the Cullinan I or the Great Star of Africa. At over 530 carats, it's so magnificent that it doesn't even seem real. And that's just one of the many spectacular jewels set in beautifully crafted pieces. These are the most treasured possessions of the British royal family.

A king in the ancient Near East would possess many pieces of gold and silver, many gems and jewels, many horses, servants, and houses, even many wives. But out of his entire treasury, some things were considered more valuable by the king. That's what the phrase "treasured possession" refers to. God essentially says to his people, "Out of all the nations, you will be the one I value most." They are that special to him. What an amazing message to believe about themselves.

"A KINGDOM OF PRIESTS." God now tells his people that they will be for him "a kingdom of priests." I don't think the people saw this one coming. They weren't priests. They were brickmakers, shepherds, bakers, and weavers. A priest in the ancient Near East was a holy man, someone who created a bridge between a god and his people. Normal folks don't know how to stand between God and anyone. How could they possibly be a kingdom of priests?

God isn't saying that every person will serve in the tabernacle like the sons of Aaron. They won't wear fancy robes and offer the sacrifices brought to God. Notice that when God gives the rationale for making them a kingdom of priests, he refers to the whole world as his. That includes all the other nations. The point is this: as a nation, they will act as a mediator between God and all of the other nations. Just as a priest mediates the commands of God to the people and the worship of the people back to God, this new nation will communicate to the world what God is like and how to worship him. And if anyone from any nation wants to worship the One True God, they will be able to do it through God's people. As a nation, Israel will be the mediator between God and all other nations.

We need mediators to help us understand how to navigate the world we live in. If we are living in a land not our own, we need local people to help us know how to accomplish the basic tasks of life: how to find and purchase food, get from place to place, take care of legal matters, and, most importantly, build relationships. Even in our own countries, we might find ourselves in places where we don't know the lingo and the ways to get something done. In a courtroom, for example, we may not know when or where to sit, stand, speak, and be quiet. A courtroom has its own set of rules and traditions. We can feel out of place, even foolish, in a place like that. We need a mediator, someone who can translate what's going on around us and tell us how to accomplish what we've come there to do.

God's people translate God to the world: his character, his commands, his love, his mighty acts of redemption. The nations of the world cannot know him unless God's people become a kingdom of priests. And if Israel lives out its identity as a kingdom of priests, that would make them truly unique among all the other nations. Priests are servants. As a kingdom of priests, Israel would be a kingdom not run by conniving, power-hungry politicians but by servants committed to making God's presence known throughout all the earth. Israel would be a servant nation instead of a ruling nation. No other kingdom in the ancient Near East takes that posture.[2] Indeed, God's people are unique.

"A HOLY NATION." God also promises his people they will be "a holy nation." That sort of makes sense. Priests were holy men and women, so the nation they lead ought to be holy. But how can a nation be holy? And in this setting, what does *holy* even mean?

The Hebrew word translated "holy" means "set apart." We know that God is holy, completely separate from creation. He exists apart from creation and is not dependent upon it in any way. God's holiness makes him, in the language of theologians, "wholly other." In plain speech that means there is no one like him.[3] We cannot know God if we do not know him as holy. In fact, "holy" is the only attribute of God repeated three times without pause: "Holy, holy, holy" cry the angelic beings who praise God in his heavenly throne room (Isaiah 6:1–4; Revelation 4:8).

Nothing and no one is holy in the sense that God is holy. But he designates other things as holy in the Bible. For example, objects used in the tabernacle by the priests were set apart from daily use and used only in the execution of the sacrifices. They were deemed holy because they were set apart for special purposes in the worship of God. Anything deemed holy is designated solely for God. And in this sense, holy takes on the meaning of sacred. And because things deemed holy will be used in the presence of God, they cannot have any defects or impurities. That adds the sense of purity to the meaning of *holy*.

I'm not sure most of us are comfortable with this understanding of holy. For example, we don't particularly like things that are set apart and made inaccessible to us. In fact, when we know that something is off limits, what's our first instinct? Figure out a way to gain access to it! And no one likes someone who's "holier-than-thou." You know the type. They want to make sure you know they are morally superior to you. You probably didn't wake up this morning wanting to spend the day with a self-righteous, sanctimonious hypocrite, did you?

Whether we're comfortable with it or not, God commands his people, "Be holy because I, the LORD your God, am holy" (Leviticus 19:2; 1 Peter 1:16). Boy, that's a bombshell of a command. Most of us don't list "holy" as the first attribute in our résumé. But being a "holy nation" doesn't mean that God's people will never sin. The Bible makes it patently clear that we're really good at sinning. God anticipated that we would make a mess of things, so the Law contained provisions for us to have our sins forgiven through offering sacrifices.

So, if being a "holy nation" doesn't mean God's people will be sinless, what does it mean? It means that God has uniquely set apart his people from all the other nations to fulfill a special purpose. All the nations are his but Abraham's descendants will have a unique character and play a unique role. God is saying to his people, "You will be a nation set apart for me to display my character to all the nations." God's people are to abandon the way of life they learned in Egypt and abstain from the way of life they will encounter in Canaan (Leviticus 18:1–5; 20:22–24). Their way of life and values will distinguish them from other nations, if they live according to the Law God gives them.

That's why the Ten Commandments are so critical. They describe the way of life that will make Israel a "holy nation." And like the role the Constitution of the United States of America plays in our legal system, the Ten Commandments establish the foundation for every law and regulation (all 613 of them!) that God gives Israel. God's Law, because it is an expression of his character, is itself holy (Romans 7:12). God's Law is set apart from the law codes of other nations. It lays out a distinct way of life that will distinguish God's people from their neighboring nations. In the Law, God places upon his people unique social, political, and ethical demands that set them apart as his and his alone.[4]

Sabbath laws provide a good example. These laws require Israel to cease all work one day out of every seven (Exodus 20:8). But that's not all. Every seventh year, Israel is also required by law not to plant or reap for an entire year (23:10–11). And if that isn't incredible enough, God's Law also requires that his people not plant or harvest every forty-ninth and fiftieth year. In this special fiftieth year, the Year of Jubilee, not only do they not work the fields, sow, or harvest, they are also to forgive the debts of those who became indebted to them and return to freedom those who have become their slaves (see Leviticus 25). In this way the nation could be economically and socially re-leveled. The Year of Jubilee was intended to "reboot" the life of the nation, to set things right that had gone awry. No other nation did this.

In an agrarian society each year's harvest was critical for the prosperity, even perhaps the survival, of the people. That makes observing a Sabbath year, and especially two years in a row when the Year of Jubilee comes around, seem foolish. Yet, God promised to prosper the nation if they obeyed his Law. As a result, when other nations see that Israel does not plant or harvest for an entire year or two and still prospers, they will interpret that prosperity as the provision of Israel's God. Israel's obedience to the Law of God makes them a showcase of the magnificence of their God (Deuteronomy 4:5–8).[5]

When we lived in Vienna, Austria, we enjoyed walking the narrow, cobbled streets of the inner city. Along those streets one could find the shops of skilled artisans, many of whom practiced the craft of their ancestors going back several generations. These artisans would put their finest goods in the front windows of their shops. Crystal, leather, silver, Viennese enamel, jewelry, pastries, and chocolates filled the storefront windows, showcased the skill of the craftsmen, and drew shoppers into the store.

God's people are a showcase people, called to a way of life that displays the skill and character of our Creator. And, like those beautiful showcase creations in Vienna, we are to be a people whose way of life is so beautifully distinct that it draws others to come in and meet the one who created us. Every act of obedience, every act of worship, every act of service, demonstrates the character of our God. Our family life, our work, our play, our hospitality, our eagerness to help others—God uses all of our life to showcase what it means to have the story of redemption emblazoned on our hearts.

A "So That" People

The description of God's people in Exodus 19:4–6 is repeated almost verbatim in 1 Peter 2:9. Writing to small groups of believers who lived in a culture hostile to their beliefs and values, Peter reminds them that they, like the nation of Israel, are a "chosen people, a royal priesthood, a holy nation, God's special possession." The repetition of this description demonstrates continuity in the identity and character of God's people in the Old and New Testaments. Peter encourages these believers to remember who they are, but even more importantly, he also reminds them *why* they are who they are. The purpose for which God has made them who they are, he writes, is "[so] that you may declare the praises of him who called you out of darkness into his wonderful light."[6] We are a "so that" people; a people created for a purpose much larger than our own salvation and our own blessing. We are who we are for the purpose of shouting, announcing, telling, communicating, broadcasting, and revealing the character and mighty acts, the power, and the grace and mercy[7] of our magnificent Redeemer who has rescued us from ignorance and brought us into a knowledge of the truth.

Peter plows on in verse 10: "Once you were not a people, but now you are the people of God; once you had not received mercy, but now you have received mercy." We were nobodies; now we're somebodies. We were helpless; now we've received all that we need. God did that for us. And he did it so that through us everyone may know the power of the cross and the wonder of redemption.

Let's get back above tree line and look out upon the majestic landscape of God's presence and work in human history. The big story of the Bible is told through God's people as we live out and live into his redemptive mission. Think about that. If we see ourselves as God's special and unique people, chosen to declare to the world just how marvelous our Redeemer is, we see ourselves in the story of the Bible. That self-understanding gives us a sense of worth and purpose we can find nowhere else. And the great news is this: God uses broken people, limited people, weak people, all kinds of people to accomplish his mission. People just like you and just like me.

The question isn't whether we are involved in God's redemptive mission—if we are God's people, we have been enlisted into that mission from the moment we were redeemed. We are a "so that" people whose identity is grounded in our participation in God's mission. We should never wonder whether we are an integral part of that mission. The question is whether we are committed to it wholeheartedly.

9

SHAPED

Really good questions catch us off guard. They make us pause and engage our brains before activating our tongues. Really good questions make the best currency for learning. As a professor I'm used to asking questions. But when a student asks a really good question, my ears perk up. Learning is threatening to break out in that classroom!

A Questionable Life?

Really good questions don't have to be complex. They don't have to be full of fancy words. In fact, the best questions use everyday words in ways that strike deep chords of meaning and significance. They kind of sneak up on you and the next thing you know, they've popped you right between the eyes. Your thoughts start churning and your heart beats a little faster. You want to say something but the first words that come to mind just seem too trivial to matter. So, you stew on it for a while. And the question comes back to you at the oddest moments. And you can't let go of it.

"What's that book about?" was that kind of question for me.

I encountered another one recently: "Are you living a questionable life?"[1]

I heard a speaker pose this question. It startled me. First, I had to figure out what he meant by "questionable." That word can mean suspicious or dubious, like "Am I living in a way that causes people to doubt whether I'm honest?" But that's not the way he was using "questionable." He wanted us to ask ourselves, "Am I living a life that makes people ask the question, 'What's different about you?'"[2]

What a thought-provoking question. It feels a little intrusive and a lot convicting. God's people are supposed to be different. And if folks aren't asking us why we're different, then we're probably not living out our identity and calling as the people of God's mission. We are called to be questionable people. Different enough to be intriguing. Consistent enough to be credible. Hospitable enough to be compelling. Sacrificial enough to be confounding. Present enough to be approachable. Redemption makes us that way and then God shapes us to live in ways that nudge people to ask, "What's different about you?"

The Shaping of a Nation

Most of the text of the Old Testament narrates how God shapes his nation to be the people of his mission. It's a fascinating story full of characters who seem as familiar as the person we see in the mirror every morning and others who seem like they walked off the set of a Hollywood fantasy. Kings, giants, and prophets; seers, priests, and warriors; widows, midwives, and children—what's not to like about a story with that kind of diverse cast?

Of course, the main character, the one true God, is always present, driving the story forward. The Bible never masks the heart of God even though at times it doesn't necessarily tell us how to read his mind. We know him through his actions and emotions. He loves, grieves, and gets angry. He leads, guides, protects, instructs, warns, and judges his people. At times it seems like he has given up on them. But God never gives up on his people.

We all know parents who won't give up on their children. Like the mom who agonizes in prayer for a child who has walked away from the faith and the dad who keeps visiting his incarcerated son, God never gives up on his people. He doesn't give up on them because he never gives up on his mission. It flows from his heart for the world.

That doesn't mean the relationship between God and his people was always smooth sailing. Nope. The opposite is true. Like stormy seas their relationship had its ups and downs. The way the Bible tells it, more downs than ups. God never gave up on his people, but they gave up on him time and again. Most of the nation of Israel's story describes how God works in, among, against, and with his people to shape them into the people he created them to be. Like a good physical trainer, he directs them, pushes them, calls out their mistakes, corrects them, feeds them, treats their wounds, and makes sure they have time to recover.

I am neither an athlete nor the son of an athlete. But I have tried to stay in shape throughout my life. Several years ago, I decided to start some weight training at the gym. It turned out that the young man who would orient me to the weight room was a student of mine. He had been an offensive lineman at a Division I university. The guy clearly still worked out. He was in shape; I wasn't. While I was struggling to do bench presses with a pitifully small amount of weight on the bar, my student looked at me and said in a Southern accent as thick and creamy as whipped butter, "Doctor Young, all my life I worked on my body and neglected my mind. It's obvious you did the opposite."

I needed to get in shape. So did Israel. God had to shape his people to live out their identity and mission. How did he do it? Three primary ways: through the Law, through the land, and through the kingdom.

THE LAW. God's people had a charter, a constitution by which they would become a nation—the Law given by God to Moses. It laid out their future in simple terms. If Israel would obey God's Law, they would prosper and become a compelling testimony to the nations of God's magnificence. If they refused to obey, God would judge them harshly and the nations would go begging, trying to find the truth about God. God didn't pull any punches with his people. Their obedience would result in a life of prosperity and security that would be the envy of all the other nations. But if they choose to chase after other gods, their life would be one of terror, famine, disease, death, captivity, and atrocities that aren't fit to be talked about in polite company. If you've got the stomach for it, read Leviticus 26 to see just how marvelous and just how awful their lives could be depending on whether they remained faithful to their God. Be sure to read all the way to the end of that chapter because the same God who promises to punish his people for disobedience also promises to never give up on them.

The Law addresses every area of life—spiritual, personal, familial, social, ethical, ritual, economic, and legal. As such, Israel's national life and culture was to be shaped by the Law. The Ten Commandments summarize the entire law code. Although comprehensive in scope, its first command is the foundation for all that follows: "You shall have no other gods before me" (Exodus 20:3). Israel struggles with this command throughout her history, and the people's refusal to remain faithful to their God alone makes it impossible for them to obey the rest of the Law. Idolatry lies at the foundation of all sin.

The writers of the Bible unflinchingly tell the story of a nation that runs after false gods and abandons God's Law. And they pay a severe price for their rebellion. God punishes the nation and, at times, they repent and return to worshiping him alone. However, idolatry has an ironlike grip on their hearts and minds. Like an addict who can't stop yearning for that which destroys them, Israel relapses into idolatry time and again. The source of God's light in the world chooses to become "part of the darkness that it had been sent to dispel."[3] To put it bluntly, Israel never becomes the enduringly faithful nation God created it to be.

Israel's failure to remain faithful to the one true God also has consequences for all the other nations. Where can they find God when his own people turn to other gods? The consequences of idolatry reach far beyond the lives of those who stray.

We already examined how God promised Abraham that his descendants would be a great nation through whom all peoples can come to know him. The Law laid the foundation for that to come true. But a nation needs more than a promise and a charter; it needs a land with defined boundaries where its citizens can dwell in peace and prosperity.

THE LAND. For most of the world's people, their ancestral homeland provides identity and security. However, that's not the case today for the almost 71 million people who have been forcibly removed from their homeland. According to the UNHCR, the United Nations agency that cares for refugees, one person is displaced from their home every two seconds as a result of conflict or persecution. Almost 30 million of these displaced people are refugees and asylum seekers.[4] Most have no hope of ever returning to the land of their families of birth. It's too dangerous. Many cannot work in the countries where they reside because it's not legal for them to do so. Millions are "hidden" residents living in the shadows in countries that do not want them. Millions are sold as slaves and trafficked. Cut off from their families and ancestral homeland, these poor souls struggle to hold on to their identity and find any sense of safety and security. They see no future where they are and no hope to return to the land of their birth and family. What a tragedy.

In the ancient Near East, land meant life. Land generated and preserved prosperity. It created an identity tied to one's ancestors, and it created security through the provision of food and generational wealth. That's why the promise and provision of a land played a central role in shaping the nation of Israel.

When God called Abraham to leave his homeland and go to the land he would show him, I doubt that Abraham thought he would be a landless wanderer for the rest of his life. Yet that's exactly what he was, someone without a permanent home whose only landholding was a burial site (Genesis 23).

Although Abraham never possesses the land, God's promise, "To your offspring I will give this land" (Genesis 12:7), remains deeply embedded in the hearts and minds of his descendants. It fortifies the resolve of the Israelites to defy Pharaoh, flee Egypt, and persevere on their arduous trek to Canaan (Exodus 6:6–8). Israel's road to fully enjoying the full blessing of the land God promised them proves to be far longer and more treacherous than anyone could have imagined. After they finally enter the land, the Israelites dwell in it but do not possess it. Instead, they live in constant tension with the inhabitants who were there before them. The struggle to drive out those inhabitants, occupy the land, and establish themselves as God's chosen nation leads to chaos and violence. This part of the Bible's story, told primarily in the books of Joshua and Judges, contains events that are far more cringeworthy than one might expect to find in a holy book. To use a highfalutin theological term favored by my grandkids, some of it is just plain "yucky."

This part of the story also raises questions that have bedeviled Bible readers for generations. Why does God command his people to destroy those already living in the land? How can we reconcile God's desire to be known and worshiped by all with his harsh treatment of the different peoples living in Canaan? These questions are troubling. Let's admit that at the beginning. But there are some important points to consider before we indict God's character and purpose. First, we need to remember that because God is just, he always judges sin. Everyone's sin. The Amorites and other nations that inhabited the land had created cultures of stunning violence, injustice, and idolatry.[5] God's justice demands that he judge their sin.

Second, God gives people a chance to repent before he executes the punishment for their sin. When Israel reaches the Promised Land, God's reputation has already made the rounds. Because of what he had done for his people on the journey out of Egypt and through the wilderness of Sinai—defeating the most powerful nation on the face of the earth, sustaining his people in a harsh environment, and destroying those who sought to destroy them—the Amorite and Canaanite kings were afraid of Israel's God. They had heard what God does to those who oppose his people (Joshua 5:1). By making himself known on the journey to Canaan, God gives those living in the land an opportunity to turn to him in worship. He is not cruel. In his mercy, God offers them an opportunity to repent and, in his grace, he offers them life. If the rulers of the peoples of Canaan had responded in worship rather than defiance, the story of Israel's conquest of the land would have been very different.

Rahab is a striking example of a Canaanite who had heard about Israel's God and feared what he would do to her city of Jericho (Joshua 2:9, 11). She knows that no one can stand against Israel's God and her fear turns into faith. Because of her faith, she is spared when the Israelites destroy Jericho. Because of her faith, she is incorporated into the people of God and, amazingly, is included in the genealogy of Israel's Redeemer, Jesus (Matthew 1:5). And because of her faith, she is included in the list of those whose lives of faith we are to imitate (Hebrews 11:13). When fear of the Lord turns to faith, it leads to life. When that fear turns into defiance, it leads to death.

In spite of the opposition of the Canaanites and the hardship of settling a new land, Israel's tribes begin to take possession of it. Their physical presence represents the presence of God. If they live into and live out their identity as a kingdom of priests and a holy nation, they will be a place for the nations to find God. In the land, Israel can begin to live according to the charter God gave them and enjoy the prosperity God promised them. In the land, they can demonstrate to the nations what it means to live in relationship with the one true God. In the land, the world can become "what it is supposed to be according to God's plan."[6] The land is to be a place where God dwells with his people and creates a nation unlike any other.

But why the land of Canaan? Why not somewhere else? In 1973, former Israeli premier Golda Meir wondered about these questions as well. She said, "Let me tell you something that we Israelis have against Moses. He took us 40 years through the desert in order to bring us to the one spot in the Middle East that has no oil."[7] In spite of Meir's witty comment, the land God chooses for his people has everything they need to become an abundantly prosperous nation.[8] God sets Israel up to succeed. And when Israel prospers, her neighbors take note of her God. That's why God chooses this place for his people. Israel sits in one of the most strategic crossroads on the planet.

Standing on Mount Carmel during a recent tour of Israel, our guide, a retired colonel from the Israeli Defense Forces, described just how strategic the land of Israel remains today. It connects three continents by land—Africa, Asia, and Europe—and provides a port for passage by sea to the Atlantic Ocean. It also contains a crucially important fresh water source, the Jordan River and the Sea of Galilee. All of the great powers of the ancient Near East recognized the importance of this land. That's why they have fought over it for centuries.

Throughout her history, the nation of Israel has been right in the middle of the rising and falling of many nations in the region (see Ezekiel 5:5). God put them exactly where they needed to be in order to become what he created them to be. "If God wanted to protect the chosen people of Israel, keep them safe from harm, one could not have chosen a worse place to put them. If, on the other hand, God wanted a people to come into contact with all the nations of the world, there are few places on this planet more suited for the purpose."[9] Because God desires to be known by all and because his people are the means whereby he makes himself known, he establishes his people in a place where they can prosper in plain sight of all the nations. God even uses latitude and longitude to execute his redemptive mission.

THE KINGDOM. "What do you want to be when you grow up?" We've all asked a kid that question. Like chicken pox and a toothless grin, answering it is a rite of passage for kids. Do you remember how you answered? I'm pretty sure my answers changed on a regular basis, but two kept coming back throughout my childhood: astronaut and truck driver. Actually, astronaut was my fallback position in case I couldn't become a truck driver. In a recent survey of more than one thousand kids under the age of twelve, the top five answers were doctor, veterinarian, engineer, police officer, and teacher.[10] It's amazing to me that truck driver didn't make that list!

I suspect that a lot of us ended up becoming something that wasn't on the top of our list when we were kids. And that's probably a good thing. As kids we can only imagine what it must be like to work as a doctor or an airline pilot or a ballerina. And, fortunately, our dreams often get dragged back to reality as we get older.

I've often wondered what the people of God thought it

would be like for them to become what God promised them they would be—his treasured possession, a kingdom of priests, and a holy nation. There were no role models for this kind of nation. None. In fact, the nation God described probably didn't really make much sense to them. No doubt, those early years in the land deromanticized whatever image they may have held on to since the Lord gave them that beautiful vision of their future back on Mount Sinai. It's hard to see yourself as a treasured possession when you're fighting for your life. It's difficult to serve as a priest to nations that are trying to wipe you off the face of the earth. It's hard to be holy when everyone is doing what seems right in their own eyes.[11] God had laid out a vision for his people that just didn't square with the harsh realities of their life. Visions don't create social order, governments do.

It's not surprising, therefore, that the people of Israel decide they need a king to help them mature into a fully functioning nation (1 Samuel 8:5). God had told his people they would have a king. But if they are to be a nation unlike any other, they must have a king unlike any other. Unlike every other king, Israel's king must submit to a higher authority, the Lord himself. Their king must not use his power to accumulate wealth at the expense of his people. He must not take advantage of the Israelites and conscript them to military service for the expansion of his realm. Israel's king must never worship other gods, and he must follow the Law reverently and completely (Deuteronomy 17:14–20). In essence, Israel's true king is their God, and the earthly king must obey the divine king. No other nation had a king like that.

But that's not the kind of king the people of Israel demand. They want a king like the kings other nations have. Even worse, they want to be a nation like all the other nations (1 Samuel 8:5, 19). In demanding an earthly king, they reject the Lord as their king, indicting him as incompetent and unable to make them into a great nation. That's blasphemy, pure and simple. No wonder the people later realize that their request for a king was an evil thing (1 Samuel 12:19).

In his mercy, God does not destroy them when they make this foolish demand. He grants their request for an earthly king. And in his grace, he lays before them the opportunity to prosper. Their choice remains the same: obey the Lord and prosper or reject him and suffer. That will be their earthly king's choice as well. Israel's history makes that patently clear. Kings who submit to the Lord's authority create prosperity for the people; those who chase after false gods bring calamity upon the people.

God sure is patient with his people. He simply will not give up on them (1 Samuel 12:22). He isn't finished with Israel because his mission isn't finished. The nations still need to know him, and his people are still the way for them to find him.

An Everlasting Dynasty

When a shepherd boy named David is anointed as king, the story intensifies and hope arises that Israel will find the prosperity that has eluded them and become the nation God intended them to be (1 Samuel 16). Let's be honest about David, however. Like all of us, he is a hot mess of inconsistencies and contradictions. At times, a man after God's own heart. But, at other times, a man who pursues the lusts of his own heart with tragic consequences. And it's not just David's personal failings and family drama that define his reign as king. The nation also finds itself in turmoil through conflict with other nations, internal divisions, and palace intrigue. The nation's character mirrors its king's. It too is a hot mess of inconsistencies and contradictions most of the time.

We have to get above tree line to make sense of the large section of the Old Testament devoted to the history of the nation of Israel and her kings.[12] Otherwise, we'll get lost in the details. Let's remember why God is establishing the kingdom of Israel. Two reasons: (1) he is faithfully fulfilling his promises to his people, and (2) he is faithfully pursuing his mission to all peoples. Through the king, God desires to shape his people into a kingdom that can fully enjoy his blessing and fully display his character to all peoples.

The high point of David's reign as king comes in a stunning promise from God: "Your house and your kingdom will endure forever before me; your throne will be established forever" (2 Samuel 7:16). A dynasty that will last forever? No king could ever ask for more than that. God's commitment to David is firm. He will establish a kingdom through David that will endure forever. No king's reign lasts forever. Death stalks both kings and paupers with the same certain outcome. But God isn't promising David that he will rule forever. The kingdom he is establishing through David will endure forever.

The significance and scope of this promise humble David. He recognizes that a kingdom established by God has consequences for all people. He acknowledges that this kingdom is "instruction for mankind" (2 Samuel 7:19 ESV), a notoriously difficult phrase to translate into English. Essentially, the phrase indicates that David sees God establishing a kingdom that will teach all humanity how to live in relationship with the one true God.[13]

God's promise that David's throne will endure forever gets off to a good start with Solomon. But in spite of Solomon's incredible prosperity and success as a king early in his reign, by the end, his reign suffers from idolatry, violence, betrayal, and division. What kind of "instruction" for all humanity is that kind of kingdom? Moreover, none of the earthly kings who follow Solomon truly fulfill David's hope that Israel would teach the nations how to know their God.

The rightful heir to David's throne, and the only one who can fulfill God's promise of an eternal kingdom, is the Redeemer, Jesus Christ. Through him God fulfills his promise to David and David's hope for the kingdom. And through the kingdom Jesus establishes, the redemptive mission of God is accomplished. Those who believe in Jesus become a part of his kingdom, redeemed by his death, submitting to his rule, and executing his mission. This kingdom is unlike any earthly kingdom, and it shows all earthly kingdoms the way to know the one true God (John 18:36). It encompasses people from every nation, tribe, people, and language, all worshiping Jesus as their king. It gives me goose bumps to imagine what it will be like when we see this kingdom in its fullest (Revelation 7:9).

That All Peoples May Know

God shapes a nation for the nations, his people for all peoples. Everything he does in, to, for, with, and against his people is done for their benefit and for the sake of the nations. God uses the Law, the land, and the kingdom to stabilize and prosper his people so that he can be known among the nations. We know that, ultimately, this purpose will be accomplished through the reign of Jesus Christ. But was this purpose ever accomplished during the time of the Old Testament? Does Israel under its earthly kings ever live up to their identity as the people of God's mission? Do people not directly descended from Abraham come to know Abraham's God through the nation?

Yes! In spite of Israel's struggle to remain faithful to God, we know that people who are not descendants of Abraham become a part of the nation and worship Israel's God. We've already talked about Rahab. And there are others. Caleb, whose father, Jephunneh, is a Kenizzite, and Uriah, the Hittite, both play important roles in the history of Israel. We also know that the Queen of Sheba comes from a distant land[14] because she has heard of Solomon's wealth and wisdom. Solomon's efforts to live out a "questionable" life provoke the queen's visit and her hard questions. Imagine her surprise as she discovers why Solomon's life and reign were different from other kings—Solomon's God.

After her audience with the king, she publicly acknowledges that Israel's prosperity and strength come from Solomon's relationship with the Lord (1 Kings 10:1). She praises Israel's God and speaks of his love for his people.

Because God blesses his people abundantly when they obey him, his fame spreads far beyond Israel's borders. And the nations come to worship him. A beautiful example of the way God draws people to himself through his people is found in Solomon's prayer at the dedication of the temple in Jerusalem.

> As for the foreigner who does not belong to
> your people Israel but has come from a distant
> land because of your name—for they will hear
> of your great name and your mighty hand and
> your outstretched arm—when they come and
> pray toward this temple, then hear from heaven, your dwelling place. Do whatever the foreigner asks of you, so that all the peoples of the
> earth may know your name and fear you, as do
> your own people Israel, and may know that this
> house I have built bears your Name.
>
> (1 Kings 8:41–43)

What a powerful, unexpected, and revealing prayer. Solomon is aware that the Lord's reputation has reached to other lands. He asks the Lord to hear the prayer of non-Israelites just as he hears the prayers of Abraham's descendants so that all peoples may know his name. Solomon clearly understands God's heart for all peoples and Israel's role in executing his mission.

God shapes a nation for the nations. Through the Law, he shows them how to create a unique way of life that will separate them from all other nations. Through the land and the kingdom, God stabilizes and prospers the people so that other nations will want to know Israel's God. God shapes his people through prosperity and victory but also through defeat and exile. Everything God does *in, for, to, with,* and *against* his people shapes them to be what God has created them to be—a "questionable" people whose lives reveal the life-giving character and presence of their God.

10

SENT

When a story captivates us and causes us to reflect on our own lives, it's the characters who do the heavy lifting. We're fascinated by how they react to events and relate to one another, how they change over time, and how they feel about what is happening around them. We develop emotional bonds with the characters in a story. Those bonds, in large measure, help make reading such an enjoyable and powerful experience. It's the same with movies. Once we're bonded emotionally with characters in a film, we'll keep coming back to renew that bond and find out what's going to happen to them. That's why over the last forty years, many of us have returned to the theater nine times to see the Star Wars saga unfold!

The cast of characters in the Bible is more breathtakingly diverse and expansive than any Hollywood blockbuster. Some appear in the story for only a brief time, but they impact the plot significantly. Some create important historical and theological points of reference, such as Abraham, Moses, and David, that tie the story together. Others are mentioned in passing or included in long lists of names. Sometimes when I'm reading the Bible I wonder why God inspired the authors to include so many details—people, places, objects, amounts, dates—that seemingly have little to do with the events at hand and the rest of the big story. I don't even know how to pronounce a lot of the names, so I just skip over them when I'm reading. That's my loss. Those aren't just names; they are people whose lives, no matter how briefly mentioned, humanize the story for us.

As interesting as the individual characters and their stories may be, we have to connect with their lives in the framework of the big story of God's redemptive mission. No doubt about it, God is the main character. He pushes the narrative forward; his presence is always felt. Some of the supporting cast play adversarial roles, others are advocates who join with God in bringing the story to its conclusion. Whereas God remains the same (Hebrews 13:8), his people change, sometimes growing and sometimes regressing, throughout the story. That's what we call character development in a work of literature, and it is a key element in the power of a story.

In the previous chapters we've examined how the people of God grow and change as the story unfolds in the Old Testament. Most of our attention has been on the nation of Israel. We've seen how they at times lived into and at other times ran away from their identity as God's people. They are the *chosen* people of God, *unique* in their calling, and *shaped* by his sovereign hand to enjoy the fullness of life in relationship with their Creator and to participate in his redemptive mission.

Although some approaches to interpreting the Bible focus on the differences between the people of God in the Old Testament (Israel) and his people in the New Testament (the church), reading the Bible as one big story helps us see that there is more continuity than discontinuity between the Old and New Testaments. What God desires for his people in the Old Testament is also his desire for the people of God in the New Testament. Like Israel, the church is chosen, unique, and shaped to fulfill God's mission.

And we are also *sent*.

A Blessing and a Mission

As Jesus's disciples gathered behind a locked door in a nondescript home in Jerusalem, uncertainty pervaded the room. The one they had given their lives to had suffered the most humiliating and dehumanizing execution the Romans could employ—crucifixion. Most thought crucifixion too cruel, but the Romans cared little about what people thought and much about what would cow the masses into submission. Thankfully, Pontius Pilate had allowed Joseph of Arimathea to take down Jesus's body before the birds of prey began their hideous ritual of tearing the flesh to pieces and eating it.

When Jesus died, the disciples' world fell apart. No one expected him to die this way, even though he had told them he would. Just a few days earlier, as they neared Jerusalem with Jesus, those who knew him best believed that the appearing of the kingdom of God was imminent (Luke 19:11). The mood was jubilant. Jesus was going to establish the kingdom that generations of Jewish families had longed for. The Romans would be driven out, the Messiah would reign, and God's people would once again prosper. But all of that proved to be a pipe dream. Jesus is dead. So, they hide and descend into doubt, confusion, and fear.

They don't know how to process the news Mary Magdalene brings them from the tomb where they buried Jesus. An empty tomb lay too far beyond the boundary of their sensibilities and too close to their unvoiced hopes. So, Peter and John run to see for themselves.[1] An empty tomb now lies before them and they have to decide what to believe. Has someone taken the body, as Mary suspected? For John, seeing the empty tomb, the strips of linen, and the head cloth, brings together everything he'd seen Jesus do and heard Jesus say. In the most powerful "Aha!" moment he's ever experienced, his understanding and faith leap into the arms of hope. Jesus has conquered death itself and is alive!

Now what? Mary's report of talking with the risen Jesus adds to Peter and John's testimony. Could it be that Jesus is alive? The Jewish leaders who had forced the hand of the Romans to execute Jesus are likely still seeking vengeance against everyone who took part in this rebellion against their authority. What would keep them from tracking down each of Jesus's disciples and executing them as well?

And then Jesus shows up. He doesn't knock. He doesn't even use the door. John's gospel tells us about it:

> On the evening of that first day of the week,
> when the disciples were together, with the doors
> locked for fear of the Jewish leaders, Jesus came
> and stood among them and said, "Peace be with
> you!" After he said this, he showed them his
> hands and side. The disciples were overjoyed
> when they saw the Lord.
>
> Again Jesus said, "Peace be with you! As the
> Father has sent me, I am sending you." And with
> that he breathed on them and said, "Receive the
> Holy Spirit." (John 20:19–22)

Jesus's words "Peace be with you!" drive out the suffocating uncertainty in the room and fill it with fresh hope. His greeting bestows on them the blessing of *shalom*, "unqualified well-being," life in its fullness.[2] The one who was dead is still the one who gives life. Fear drains life from us; peace fills us up with life. And he shows them his body, pierced and bloodied. How intimate. How jarring.

Let there be no doubt: he was the one hanging on that cross. The marks of death amplify the miracle of resurrection. His voice coming from a scarred, breathing body drowns out the voices of doubt and fear that have threatened to strangle the disciples' faith.

And then he bestows upon them a mission, one that mirrors his very own. "As the Father has sent me, I am sending you." No more hiding behind locked doors. No more wondering if they will still have the joy of following him. His words encourage them. For a moment. And then uncertainty crashes the party again. Sending? Where? To do what? Right now? Being sent somewhere is the last thing they want. It feels safe in that room behind a locked door enjoying the presence of Jesus again. The thought of going outside terrifies them. But it also clarifies the life that lies before them. Yes, Jesus was sent by the Father. Sent to pick up a cross and carry it. Sent to die. Sent to redeem. Sent to bring life.

They would soon find out what it means to be sent by the Sent One. It would change their world. In fact, it would turn their world upside down (Acts 17:6 ESV). It ought to do the same with ours.

All God's People Are Sent

Growing up in a small town, everywhere I went folks knew who I was. If I showed up at the A to Z Supermarket in town to "pick up a few things," the owner, stocker, butcher, produce guy, and cashier all knew who sent me. I was Gene and Donna's boy. Enough said. When Mom sent me to the store, I had explicit instructions about what to buy. Funny how Snickers bars kept mysteriously ending up in the paper sack I carried home on my bike, even though they weren't on the list Mom gave me. But I made sure the things on that list ended up in the sack too. I had been sent on a mission by someone I loved dearly and wanted to please.

Jesus was also sent on a mission by one whom he loved and whose will he desired to fulfill. That's why one of the primary ways the New Testament describes the relationship of the Father,

Son, and Holy Spirit is through the language of *sending*. The Father sends the Son; the Father and the Son send the Holy Spirit. In a beautiful yet mystifying way, God is both sender and the one sent.

The sending motif provides such a powerful picture of the relationship between the Father, Son, and Holy Spirit, because it bridges God's nature and mission. A lot of churches and ministries use the phrase "mission of God" to express this connection. That English phrase translates the Latin expression *missio Dei*. We can easily see the connection between the English word "mission" and the Latin *missio*. But interestingly, *missio* literally means "act of sending" in Latin. *Dei* means "God." Although "mission of God" is an accurate translation of *missio Dei*, the Latin phrase more literally means the "sending of God" or the "sentness of God."

Sending implies *movement*. In the Bible, God's movement is always outward and toward humanity. He makes the first move in his relationship with us. He takes the initiative and steps toward us. Always has. Always will. God's movement toward humanity expresses his eternal love and is driven by his will to be known and worshiped by all. God cannot be known unless he makes himself known by moving toward us. Because he moves toward us, we can respond to him.

Now here's the hard part. God's people are created to mirror God's movement. Our basic posture, just like God's, is to be outward and toward others. As the people of God's mission, we are called to make the first move. But that's contrary to our nature. Without even trying, our natural tendency, our basic instinct, is to be inwardly focused on our own needs rather than outwardly focused on the needs of others. The instinct to focus on our own needs, and to meet them even at the expense of others, has been described by the Latin phrase *homo incurvatus in se*, "humanity turned in on itself." This inward curvature of the soul lies at the foundation of our sinfulness, a direct result of the fall of humanity.[3]

As I write this chapter, we are experiencing the coronavirus pandemic of 2020. Out of fear, people are stockpiling food and other basic items. Shoppers empty store shelves of the most sought-after goods as soon as stockers fill them. Videos of people fighting over toilet paper and stealing food from another shopper's grocery cart are standard fare on news broadcasts and Facebook feeds. The basic instinct to hoard as a protection against possible deprivation, no matter the cost to someone else, has reared its ugly head and roared with an intensity that few of us have ever seen. People have turned in on themselves and lost sight of those around them. It's a natural instinct to live this way.

That's why we need Christ to turn us inside out, to fundamentally reorient our heart and soul away from the naked pursuit of our own self-interest and toward the interests of others. That's exactly what Jesus did on the cross and that's exactly what he does for us. When Christ redeems us, he saves us from ourselves and sets us free from the destructive effects of the fall, including *homo incurvatus in se*. He makes it possible for us to lead "questionable" lives—lives that seek the good of others even at the risk of our own, lives characterized by radical compassion and jaw-dropping generosity that others simply cannot ignore. Lives turned inside out turn the world upside down.

"The world needs a pastor. They just don't know it." I heard a Lutheran pastor say that recently. She's right. I can't remember a time when there was a greater sense of anxiety in our society. With almost instant access to news about what's happening anywhere in the world at any given time, our mental and emotional circuits are overloaded with images and information. And most of what we take in distresses us. We know intuitively the world isn't what we want it to be, isn't what we think it's "supposed to be," and the news cycles reinforce our intuition. We don't know what to do to fix our world, so we pursue pleasure to anesthetize our pain. And we use distraction to drown out the sense of dread that nothing we do will ultimately make a difference. Apart from Christ we have nowhere to land our yearnings for the world to be healed; nowhere to place our hope.

That's why the world needs a pastor, someone who can enter into its pain and speak words of comfort and hope. That's exactly why Jesus sends his followers into the world. In megacities and villages, slums and Wall Street, the sent people of God pastor the world, bringing hope to despair, wisdom to confusion, truth to deception, and redemption for the oppressed. A group of Jesus-following women bring healing and learning to children in one of the most broken and violent slums in the Middle East by generously giving of themselves to meet the needs of those whom others choose to ignore. A Jesus-following chaplain brings the hope of the gospel and the gift of being treated like a human being to the most violent inmates in America's federal prison system by teaching them how to express themselves through art. These believers are living inside out and turning their worlds upside down because they see themselves as the sent people of God.

All God's people are sent. We are all called to turn our lives inside out and turn our worlds upside down. And that's exactly what it means for us to live into the story of the Bible.

One Big Story, One Big Mission

During his final days with the disciples, the resurrected Jesus talks a lot about sending them out on a mission (Matthew 28:16–20; Mark 16:9–20; Luke 24:44–49; John 20:19–23; Acts 1:1–11). In these conversations, he emphasizes that the scope of the mission is universal. He uses phrases such as "all nations," "all the world," "all creation," "everywhere," and "the ends of the earth" to describe just how far his disciples are to take the good news of redemption. God's mission is "all to all to all"—all God's people sent to all peoples all over the world.

We must never see *our* mission to be narrower in scope than *God's* mission.

When Jesus walked the land of Israel, an "all to all to all" mission scandalizes those who believe the scope of redemption begins and ends with God's chosen people, the Jews. That's what the disciples believe. How could they think otherwise? Although diverse in profession, personality, politics, and religious zeal, God's chosen people know that their Jewish identity takes precedence over any of the differences they may have. They are Jewish. Jesus is Jewish. Jesus is their Messiah. A Jewish Messiah brings redemption to Jews. Everything they had been taught from the Hebrew Scriptures, their sense of history and destiny as God's chosen people, and their conviction that the nation wasn't yet what God had promised it to be supported that understanding of the Messiah's coming. Surely, they must have thought, Jesus wants them to make disciples of their fellow Jews.

And they're right. But not totally. God's desire to be known and worshiped has always been universal in scope. Out of all the other nations, he chooses Abraham and his descendants as his own people. He wants his people to know and worship him, no doubt about it. But his choice of Abraham's descendants was never just for their sakes. When Jesus sends his disciples to make disciples of "all nations" (Matthew 28:19), he uses language that reminds them of what God promised Abraham, "all peoples on earth will be blessed through you" (Genesis 12:3). And this isn't the first time Jesus has talked this way. From the very beginning of his ministry, Jesus emphasizes in his teaching that "all peoples" will be included in the blessing that Messiah brings. For example, after observing the faith of a Gentile, he notes that "many will come from the east and the west, and will take their places at the feast with Abraham, Isaac and Jacob in the kingdom of heaven" (Matthew 8:11). Jesus uses "from the east and the west" metaphorically to mean "from everywhere,"

ONE TRUE STORY, ONE TRUE GOD

not just from Israel. He makes it clear that Gentiles will enjoy the blessings brought by Messiah just like the Jewish patriarchs Abraham, Isaac, and Jacob. It has always been God's plan to bring the blessings of Messiah through his people to all peoples. Still is.

When Jesus commands his disciples to "go and make disciples of all nations" (Matthew 28:19), he makes it clear the disciples must think beyond the boundaries of their homeland. But they will likely not go on their own initiative. Like birds that need to be nudged out of the nest in order to fly, the disciples need this direct command to jolt them out of their limited view of God's mission. If they still want to follow Jesus, they must go. His command flies in the face of their sense of identity and national history.

Jesus pushes them out—out of their land, their identity, their security, their convictions, and their emotional comfort zone. His command to "go"[4] is as daunting and demanding as was the command to Abraham to leave everything and "go" to a place that he did not know (see Genesis 12:1; Hebrews 11:8). Identity is the key. If they won't leave behind their deepest convictions about identity, they will never go and make disciples. Jesus, therefore, rearranges their understanding of what it means to be the people of God. "Go" is not the main command; "make disciples of all nations" takes that honor. The sending of the disciples is more about "to whom" than "where." The goal isn't to get to as many places as possible; it's to see as many people as possible come to faith in Jesus and follow him as a disciple. That means being a follower of Jesus isn't reserved for the descendants of Abraham. Boundaries, land, and ancestry will not define God's people. Boundaries, both geographic and ethnic, must be crossed; land and identities must be left behind for the sake of establishing the new people of God.[5] That's what it means to be sent.

But the disciples aren't yet ready for that kind of mission. They need more time with the resurrected Jesus.

Waiting

None of the disciples know what it means to follow a resurrected Jesus. The last three years have been exciting, exhausting, and at times confounding. It was never boring, that's for sure. But now what? Luke tells us in the opening chapter of the book of Acts that the forty days the disciples spend with Jesus in Jerusalem after the resurrection are critical. During that time, he lives with them, eats with them, listens to them, and allows them to touch him, all convincing proofs that Jesus is indeed resurrected from the dead (Acts 1:1–3).[6] They have to be convinced of that fact or they will never embrace the mission he is sending them to accomplish. Why would they pay such a heavy price if they aren't fully convinced that Jesus has conquered death?

The resurrection changes everything. It is God's shout to them and to the world that Jesus is Lord! Lord over sin, death, and evil! Lord over all creation! Lord over angels, demons, and Satan himself! Lord over all earthly kings, rulers, and human institutions! Lord over a raggedy bunch of fearful followers! His disciples will go and make disciples of all nations because he is Lord of all. They had heard him say, "All authority in heaven and on earth has been given to me" (Matthew 28:18). Now they see, touch, and hear his authority up close and more convincingly than ever before.

Jesus had already demonstrated authority in ways that none of the disciples had ever experienced before—authority over sickness, disease, disability, and death; authority over the wind and waves; authority over evil spirits; authority to forgive sins; and authority to interpret the Scriptures unlike any other teacher. His power took their breath away. But now, having been raised from the dead, his authority takes a new place in their lives because, as Davies and Allison put it, "universal lordship means universal mission."[7]

The resurrection convinces them that Jesus's promise of full redemption, the coming of the kingdom of God, is still alive. During these forty days, Jesus makes the promised kingdom the primary topic of their conversations. And he promises they will experience the Holy Spirit's presence in a new way. They know this promise also confirms the coming of the kingdom of God (Acts 1:4–5; see also Isaiah 44:3 and Joel 2:28). These conversations intensify their longing for that day when the Romans get their due and the risen Christ makes everything that's wrong in the world right, everything that's broken whole, and everything that's ugly beautiful. Like thoroughbreds in the starting gate itching to run the race, they can hardly wait for Jesus to make it all happen.

So, they ask Jesus, "Lord, are you at this time going to restore the kingdom to Israel?" (Acts 1:6).

When we were living in Poland during Communist rule, my mother would send us care packages with food and toys for the children. Our kids didn't get to see Grandma in person, but they got to know her through those packages. In them the kids would find things we couldn't buy in Poland at that time—Snickers bars, Honey Nut Cheerios, and Gummy Bears, along with toys and clothes. She would also include cassette tapes with messages she recorded for them. Our children developed a fantasized image of what it must be like at Grandma's house.

In their minds, they would never have to eat vegetables at Grandma's house, only the goodies that she sent. There would be new toys every day and no grouchy adults around to tell them "no." They had never heard Grandma say that word. What a place Grandma's house must be: no vegetables, new toys, and no adults saying "no" to them. When we told the kids one evening that we were going to Grandma's house the next day, they were so excited they barely slept all night.

We didn't tell them we had to get up long before dawn, travel by taxi to the train station, take a train for five hours to the capital city, wait two hours in the airport, fly eight hours to the United States, wait two hours in another airport and then take another two-hour flight and a short car trip to Grandma's house. We didn't tell them that.

After we got them up in the middle of the night and rushed to the station, counted heads and suitcases for the tenth time, and finally sat down in our compartment, the train pulled out. We hadn't been moving for fifteen minutes when the oldest of our children asked the question children all over the world ask, "Are we there yet?" They just couldn't wait to get to Grandma's.

In the same way, the disciples couldn't wait to get into the kingdom Jesus promised. Just like our kids, their anticipation of just how wonderful everything would be when the risen Christ establishes the kingdom makes them ask, "Are we there yet? Is now the time when we get to enjoy all that we've been looking forward to?"

Jesus's answer disappoints them: "It is not for you to know the times or dates the Father has set by his own authority."[8] In other words, "No, we are not there yet. And don't worry about it. We'll get there; it will happen. But knowing when it's going to happen is above your pay grade!"

It is not yet time to consummate God's redemptive purpose. The mission of God isn't finished, and the disciples still aren't ready to be sent on his mission.

Empowered for Mission

Jesus plows ahead, "But you will receive power when the Holy Spirit comes on you; and you will be my witnesses in Jerusalem, and in all Judea and Samaria, and to the ends of the earth" (Acts 1:8). He gives the disciples both a promise and a mandate. They cannot fulfill the mission without the empowerment of the Holy

Spirit. But they will receive it, Jesus promises, and that will make all the difference in the world.

But what does it mean to be empowered by the Spirit? The Greek word Luke uses in this verse for "power" generally describes a visible manifestation of God's presence and work. It's often associated with signs and miracles in the book of Acts. And that's exactly what the disciples experience as they step out in mission. They see the Spirit heal and work miracles that cannot be explained away by skeptics and scoffers. Miracles confirm that God is with them and the gospel they preach is true. They strengthen the disciples' faith and embolden them to keep telling the story of the risen Christ. Luke fills the book of Acts with stories of the miraculous work of the Holy Spirit through the disciples.

Let's admit it. There's a lot of disagreement among Christians about how we experience the presence and power of the Holy Spirit. That's a pity. One thing we can know for sure is that the primary work of the Spirit is to point people to Jesus. That's exactly what Jesus said the Spirit would do (John 15:26). And that's exactly what Jesus tells the disciples the Spirit will empower them to do. Performing miracles is not their mission. Telling the story of the one who died on the cross for their sins and was raised from the dead—that's their mission and that's what the Spirit will empower them to do while they wait for Jesus to come back and establish his kingdom on earth. The New Testament—from the book of Acts through the book of Revelation—narrates how the people of God, empowered by the Spirit of God, testify to the risen Son of God and fulfill the mission of God to the ends of the earth. Now that's a story worth reading and a story worth adopting as our own!

Like the disciples, we live between the first and second comings of Christ. And like them, we are empowered by the Holy Spirit to point people to Jesus. That's our mission. That's why we're still on this planet. As one Baptist preacher told me, "When we baptize people, we don't hold 'em down until they go straight to heaven because God has something for them to do here!"

The mission is clear—"be my witnesses"—and expansive—"to the ends of the earth." That sounds daunting to Jesus's disciples. Sounds daunting to me too. But the authority of the risen Christ and the power of the Holy Spirit make it possible for all of us to be about his mission.

All God's people are sent.

11

EXILED

"**D**ad, who am I? Am I an American? Am I a Pole?" When your twelve-year-old son asks a profound and heartfelt question, you pay attention.

We were flying from Wrocław, Poland, where we had lived for seven years, to the capital city to catch a flight back to the United States. It had been a year since we'd moved from our home in Poland to live and work in the States. In his twelve years of life, he had lived in seven different houses in five different cities, and in three different countries on two continents. That tally doesn't include numerous nights spent in hotels and in friends' and family members' homes. During the seven years we had lived in Poland, he had learned to speak Polish fluently, often being mistaken for a native speaker, and built a tight network of Polish friends through the local elementary school that he attended. All of our close relationships were with Poles.

Leaving Poland the year before had been a physically and emotionally draining experience for all of us. And our first year living in the United States had been the most difficult of our lives. We felt like immigrants living in a country not our own. But we buckled down and entered into life in the suburbs of a major city. Life felt frenzied in the United States: schools, driving, work, driving, shopping, driving, sports, driving, church, driving. To us, the United States was a foreign country with a way of life and a set of cultural values that we didn't particularly understand and definitely didn't like.

That's why we jumped at the chance for him and me to return to Poland for a couple of weeks almost exactly one year after we'd left the place we called home. I'll never forget the scene when we landed at the airport in our city. Just beyond the chain link fence around the perimeter of the tarmac stood several of his former classmates waving and yelling to him as we got off the plane. Once we cleared customs the real fun began. He switched into Polish seamlessly and the parents of one of his closest friends gathered him up, put him in their car, and drove him home. I didn't see him for the next two weeks as the families of his school friends passed him on from one home to another. We reconnected at the airport and walked to the plane with the same group of kids behind the fence waving and shouting their goodbyes.

Leaving that place a second time stung even more deeply than our departure the year before. His tearful "Dad, who am I?" came from a heart that was hurting. He felt uprooted, displaced, and disoriented, somehow cast adrift in questions of identity, relationships, and place. Our whole family did. I answered instinctively with the only thing that seemed permanent in my life.

"Son, you are a child of God."

Who Are We?

Where do we find our primary source of identity? Is it our nationality, race, politics, profession, or income level? All of these contribute to our sense of self, but they are only partial descriptions of who we are. Unfortunately, we draw lines around these traits to separate ourselves from others. But Jesus's followers have an identity that sits above these traits and rules over them. Our primary identity is being redeemed followers of Jesus, the people of God's mission. We are God's people before we are anything else. Our identity is based in our confession of the Redeemer, Jesus Christ. In him there are no distinctions in nationality, ethnicity, gender, and social status. Paul says it this way:

> So in Christ Jesus you are all children of God
> through faith, for all of you who were baptized
> into Christ have clothed yourselves with Christ.
> There is neither Jew nor Gentile, neither slave
> nor free, nor is there male and female, for you
> are all one in Christ Jesus.   (Galatians 3:26–28)

In Christ Jesus we are all children of God. Just start there when you think about identity. And stay there. That's how we can put all of the ways we like to distinguish and separate ourselves from one another in the garbage bin of Satan's lies. God has chosen us (all of us who name Christ as Savior) to be his people, shaped us (all of us) to be unique among all the peoples of the earth, and sent us (all of us) to make himself known. We belong to Christ Jesus first—not to a church, a denomination, or a theological tradition, much less a political agenda, a social class, or a profession.

Wouldn't it be powerful if those who know us well see us this way? What if the first thing people who know us say is, "I know them. They are followers of Jesus." To the degree that we are known primarily by anything other than our faith in Jesus Christ, our idolatries are revealed. Because we've given ourselves to other identities first, we are idolaters. For example, if we are known more for our politics than the gospel, we are worshiping the gods of power and privilege more than Jesus. If we are known more for condemning those who have chosen a different life-style than the forgiveness of sins accomplished on the cross, we are worshiping the god of arrogant self-righteousness more than Jesus. That's a hard word, but true. It forces me to ask my-self every day, "Who do people say that I am?"[1]

Why We Are Who We Are

In an earlier chapter we looked at the way the apostle Peter uses the language of Exodus 19:4–6 to describe who we are. In 1 Peter 2:9 he describes us as "a chosen people, a royal priesthood, a holy nation, God's special possession." Peter makes it clear that we are who we are so that we might make known the One who made us who we are. We are a "so that" people, transformed from dark-ness into his wonderful light—from being ignorant to knowing him. We, who were not a people at all, Peter goes on, have been made into the showcase people of God—from nobodies into somebodies, from those who had not experienced God's mercy to those who have, from being objects of wrath to being trophies of grace (1 Peter 2:9–10).

God did not make his people to be isolated icons of his image. We are called, shaped, and sent to be present among others, to live among others as his representatives, agents of his redemptive mission. God has shaped us to make known the virtues, the ex-cellences, the praises of the one who called us into existence as a people, the Lord Jesus himself. As one biblical scholar puts it, our raison d'être is to be a special people "who make known what God has done, displaying his power, grace, and mercy."[2] To put it more simply, we have one reason to live—to make Christ known.

We Are a Displaced People

Being a sent people implies that we live with a sense of being uprooted, displaced, and somehow distant from the culture in which we reside. We are like exiles living in a place not fully our home. As such, we live with a sense of always being an outsider looking in, fully present but not fully belonging.

Life during the coronavirus pandemic has created an odd sense of being present while still distant. Social distancing separates us, but technology allows us to continue to relate to one another. We are together, sort of. One powerful video I saw captures the strange reality of being together, but not really. A young woman holds up her left hand and points excitedly at the glittering diamond on her ring finger. She and her fiancé are beaming and jumping with excitement. She's telling her elderly grandfather she is engaged! And he is delighted as well. He's quarantined in a care facility and they are standing outside his room on the lawn. He places his right hand on the pane of glass that separates them while tears stream down his face. She reaches out and places her hand on the other side of the glass to match his. He's there with them, entering into their joy, but in a painfully ironic way, he is really an outsider looking in, unable to experience the moment with them. As God's chosen, unique, shaped, and sent people, we will always be outsiders in this world.

You remember that God's initial call to Abraham occurs in Mesopotamia where his family worships false gods (Joshua 24:2–3). God commands Abraham to abandon the very foundations of his life, everything that is familiar to him including his gods and his home. Abraham obeys, leaves everything, and becomes a landless wanderer, an immigrant, in the land of Canaan, worshiping the Lord. For more than sixty years, Abraham lives a seminomadic life, moving from region to region without owning land, residing as something of a guest in regions owned and controlled by others. During this time, he describes himself as a "foreigner and stranger" (Genesis 23:4). His obedience to God's command, his willingness to leave everything and become a wanderer, means that his identity is primarily grounded in his God. And as the Lord blesses him, others see the character and power of Abraham's God.

Through most of their history, God's chosen people live as exiles—in Egypt, in the wilderness of Sinai, in Assyria, in Babylon, and even in the land of Canaan. In each place, they are to hold fast to their God and the way of life he calls them to. They can do that no matter where they physically reside. Doing so, however, will distinguish them from those among whom they live. They are outsiders.

Peter identifies those who follow Jesus Christ as "foreigners and exiles" (1 Peter 2:11). He knows from personal experience that being sent on mission by the risen Christ causes you to live as resident aliens, expatriates, immigrants—those who are present yet somehow separate—no matter where you reside. If the sent people of God choose to live according to the values and beliefs of his kingdom, their friends, neighbors, and colleagues will see they are different and wonder why. That's what it means to lead "questionable" lives. When we live out our redemption, those who know us will want to know why.

But there's a price to pay for living this way. Because resident aliens do not fully participate in the customs and practices of the nation where they are living, they do not have all the privileges and access to power that citizens enjoy. They are often misunderstood and stand as the first to be blamed for any misfortune that might befall their communities. They are watched closely, critically, and suspiciously by those around them, and they are often taken advantage of. In some communities, they are treated with outright and open hostility. That was the experience of those believers living under Roman rule whom Peter addressed in his letter. And it is still the experience of millions of Jesus-followers around the world today.

As foreigners living in Communist Poland, the license plate

on our van was green. Vehicles owned by Polish citizens had black plates. Because fuel was scarce, we didn't drive the van very much, but when we did, our vehicle stood out like a sore thumb. People stared and pointed. The police noticed too. It seemed like they pulled us over just about every time we drove our van.

That van came to symbolize just how different we felt as we began to learn Polish and figure out how to live in our adopted home city of Kraków. Physically we looked the same as our neighbors and those we passed on the street. But as soon as we opened our mouths, everyone knew we weren't Poles. And they treated us differently. Most were patient and kind enough to try to communicate with someone who spoke Polish at a toddler level. But some just blew us off and laughed when we tried to converse with them. We didn't know how to buy groceries, how to get a haircut, or how to do most of what it takes to live. We were always on edge, aware that we were outsiders and just one phrase or act away from making fools of ourselves. We lived in Poland but we were outsiders and we did not feel "at home."

Even as our language skills grew and we figured out how to "do life" in Poland, the feeling of being an outsider never went away. We developed wonderful friendships and began to enjoy the city and beautiful countryside of southern Poland. We learned the history of our adopted homeland and developed a deep respect for the resilience and ability of the Polish people to survive through multiple wars and occupations. Slowly but surely Poland became our home. But not really. We lived in Poland for several years but we were never Polish. We developed deep friendships with Poles but, even so, we were always the outsiders, always somehow on the outside looking in, like those who don't "get" the joke that cracks everyone else up.

As foreigners and exiles, the redeemed people of God will always be, to a certain degree, cultural "outsiders." As God's chosen, unique, shaped, and sent people, we should be different from those among whom we live, even if we've lived among them our entire lives. Our way of life ought to set us apart from those around us because we are the subjects of a king and a kingdom that are "not of this world" (John 18:36).

When Jesus answers Pontius Pilate, "My kingdom is not of this world," he doesn't mean that his kingdom isn't present in this mess of a fallen world. He simply states that his kingdom is unlike any earthly kingdom because it is built on beliefs, values, and behaviors that flow from the character of God. Paul celebrates this great truth with different language by reminding the believers in Philippi that "our citizenship is in heaven" (Philippians 3:20) because our identity and lives are shaped by the resurrected Lord Jesus Christ, not by the world.

Being foreigners and exiles has far less to do with where we live than how we live. When we trust in Jesus Christ and become a part of God's sent people, we take on a new identity, new values, and a new way of life. That transformation creates a sense of dislocation from the way of life we had adopted before knowing Christ. Through that transformation, we become, in a real and powerful sense, exiles and strangers. For those who physically leave their homeland to live in a foreign land, that dislocation is intentional and obvious. But we are all God's sent people, all called to live as foreigners and resident aliens, all living in exile, even if we are living in the town where we were born.

Avoid and Embrace

How can we live a "dislocated" life in the place we've called home for our entire life? Peter tells us. Remember, he's writing to communities of believers whose distinct way of life has brought them under close scrutiny, even suspicion and hostility, from those among whom they live. He writes, "Dear friends, I urge you, as foreigners and exiles, to abstain from sinful desires, which wage war against your soul. Live such good lives among the pagans that, though they accuse you of doing wrong, they may see your good deeds and glorify God on the day he visits us" (1 Peter 2:11–12). We can summarize his message this way: the exiled people of God will be known by what they avoid and what they embrace.

Peter urges us to "abstain from sinful desires, which wage war against your soul" (v. 11). "Sinful desires" could also be translated "uncurbed human impulses"[3] or "unrestrained indulgence." We showcase our sinfulness when we take whatever we desire and utterly disregard its impact upon the lives of others. Toddlers who see a toy they want do not stop to think about the effect of their behavior on another little boy or girl when they snatch it from their grasp. When we are turned in upon ourselves, we don't care how our greed and selfish ambition affect others. At the end of the day, almost all sinful behavior, even idolatry, flows from selfishness.

The unbridled pursuit of what we want, when we want it, regardless of the consequences contradicts the believer's essential identity as a Christ-follower. Jesus modeled selflessness, the unwavering commitment to the good of others at great personal cost. That's the cost of redemption and it's a cost the redeemed must be willing to pay as well. That's why Peter describes an unwavering commitment to one's own good no matter the cost to others as contradictory to the lifestyle of a Christ-follower. Such behavior, Peter observes, "wars" against your soul.

This "soul-war" rages on two fronts. We engage the first front internally when we sense inward conflict and are tempted to give in to our impulse to sin. Our desires war against our conscience. And if we run after such unrestrained indulgence, guilt wars against our identity as the redeemed. This internal struggle is a critical indicator of the presence of the Holy Spirit in our lives. The second front in the "soul-war" is fought externally. Because we are aliens and strangers, our behavior is closely watched by others. When our lifestyle contradicts Jesus's selflessness, we war against our testimony by contradicting the character of the Redeemer. In other words, our personal and corporate godliness as the redeemed has far higher stakes than just our own relationship with God; it's a matter of the reputation of the risen Christ. When we wantonly pursue our own sinful desires, we mask our identity, contradict our message, and compromise our mission as the sent people of God.

Peter doesn't just leave us with the negative command to abstain. He goes on: "Live such good lives among the pagans that, though they accuse you of doing wrong, they may see your good deeds and glorify God on the day he visits us" (v. 12).

The people of God's mission are urged to lead a life that those outside the community of faith deem virtuous and good. By pairing this command with the previous one to resist the unbridled pursuit of one's own desires, it seems logical that the "good" life Peter envisions is one characterized by sacrifice and the intentional pursuit of the good of others. As with the previous command, we tend to think of living a good life, a virtuous life, as an issue of personal holiness for the sake of our own relationship with God. But Peter doesn't focus on that at all. He emphasizes that the fundamental issue is how the believer's life is viewed by the unbelieving world. Does it commend to them the person of Jesus and compel them to believe?

Peter assumes that believers can live in a way that unbelievers will recognize as good. He does not categorically characterize unbelieving culture as only evil and the Christian community as good. By living in ways that are consistent with their identity as God's people, yet esteemed as good by the broader culture, the believing community builds bridges of respect with those who do not yet know Christ. Peter urges the people of God's mission to be engaged fully and beneficially in the lives of those among whom they live so that they may make clear the character of the one who has redeemed them. In order to do that, we have to be constantly asking, "What are the values we share with the broader culture that allow us to build relationships, earn trust, and demonstrate the character of Jesus?"

It's always interesting to gauge people's reactions when, in response to the question "What do you do?" I answer, "I am a seminary president." More often than not, there's a puzzled expression on their face and a moment of awkward silence, before they respond, "Oh," and then leave it at that. I used to wonder if their puzzled expression means that they don't know what a seminary is or that they can't possibly imagine me being the president of anything! I gave up on wondering about that.

What comes next in the conversation makes all the difference in the world. Generosity is the key. Asking, "And you? What do you do?" is an act of generosity. It signals that we are more interested in others than in talking about ourselves. Some folks don't want to talk. That's okay. In that case, it's generous to stop talking. But it's amazing how many people enjoy telling me about their work. Americans value work, and when we give folks the opportunity to tell us about something they value, they feel valued themselves. Making others feel that you are more interested in them than in telling them about yourself helps build trust and respect. A generous spirit embodies the generosity of our God. It may be just what's needed for someone to ask, "What's different about you?"

I'm pretty sure I am not gifted as an evangelist. Most folks aren't. But we're not talking specifically about evangelism. All of us are a part of God's mission. When we live as foreigners and exiles, our lives create the curiosity and even the sense of value that may help someone move a little closer to faith in Christ. A friend of mine says that in every relationship we have the opportunity to help someone take another step toward Jesus. And another step.

And another, until they fall into his arms of mercy. By helping people take another step toward Jesus, we set the table for the gospel's generous feast of grace to be served.

Peter reminds us that sometimes those outside the community of believers may misunderstand why the redeemed live the way they do. In some cases, the good lives believers lead may cause unbelievers to falsely accuse them of doing wrong. The apostle Paul and his companions, for example, were accused of dishonoring the goddess Artemis and disrupting the business interests of craftsmen and merchants who made their living selling items to those who came to worship in her temple in Ephesus (Acts 19). That happens today as well. When the believing community's way of life is perceived as a threat to the economic and political interests of those in power, they can be slandered, shamed, shunned, imprisoned, and even physically attacked.

And how should we respond if that were to happen to us? Our natural desire would be to angrily defend ourselves, to fight back, to grasp for power, and even exact revenge. But that's not what Peter exhorts us to do. No matter how unbelievers respond to the good deeds of the believing community, believers must press on in doing good. Slandered, cheated, misrepresented, mocked, and ostracized—believers are to keep on doing good for the sake of, not just in spite of, those who persecute them. Responding to unjustified accusations and attacks this way models the very character and behavior of the Lord Jesus. Although he committed no crime, unjust and violent men arrested, beat, and shamed him publicly. His response? "When they hurled their insults at him, he did not retaliate; when he suffered, he made no threats. Instead, he entrusted himself to him who judges justly" (1 Peter 2:23).

Peter's confidence is that through the presence of foreigners and exiles whose identity and testimony model the selfless love of Christ, some who are not God's people will become God's people, and some who have not yet tasted God's mercy will feast upon it. And when God's redemption is complete and his kingdom fully revealed, these too will know and worship him. When we live with the certainty that such will be the case and we will have been a part of it, that's a life worth getting up for tomorrow.

Do We Know Who We Are?

Identity is the key. As foreigners and exiles, we run the double risk of losing our identity by refusing to lead lives that are any different from those around us and of distorting our identity by refusing to enter into the lives of others in ways they respect and trust. We have to fight for our identity. If we don't define ourselves, someone else will do it for us.

When we are defined by others, we are naturally put into pre-formed categories, stereotypes that others use to interpret everything that we do. Our task is to define ourselves through the way we express our faith in Jesus Christ. As New Testament scholar Scot McKnight says, "Culture cannot define or determine the parameters of the church, nor can it define its mission. When this happens, the church loses its bearings, begins to wobble, and eventually falls into a state of lethargy and ineffectiveness."[4] There's really only one way to avoid that—by living out our identity consistently and our mission without compromise. Identity and mission cannot be separated. Identity without mission creates arrogance and passivity. And mission without identity creates frenzied activity and futility.

We spend a lot of time worrying about our identity as God's people. And that's good, unless we don't see mission as an integral part of our identity. Our mission defines us more clearly than any list of beliefs and behaviors. Without mission, we cannot be what God has created us to be. "Either we are defined by mission, or we reduce the scope of the gospel and the mandate of the church."[5] Those are powerful words, ones that capture what it means for us to live into and live out the big story of God's redemptive mission.

THE QUESTION
THAT CHANGED ME

The question "What's that book about?" started me on a journey of discovery that changed the way I read the Bible. On the journey, I realized that the Bible ought to be read as a story. It has a compelling plot with twists, drama, tension, and resolution that provides structure and movement to the story. And it introduces us to an amazing cast of characters who make the story real and approachable. No matter what passage I'm reading in the Bible, I instinctively place it in the framework of the story's five threads—creation, fall, redemption, consummation, and the people of God's mission. As the plot unfolds, I see God driving the story forward toward the glorious end he has foreordained, the consummation of his redemptive mission. I love reading the Bible as a story.

That journey not only changed the way I read the Bible, it also changed me.

IT CHANGED THE WAY I SEE GOD. The Bible is unequaled among stories because it is the story of the God who is unrivaled. Unrivaled in love, in authority, in holiness; unrivaled in justice, mercy, and grace. God is bigger to me now, yet nearer and more accessible. Reading the Bible as the story of God's redemptive mission, I see God's love driving the story forward on almost every page. It focuses my attention on the cross where God's love is revealed in its fullness. And it convinces me that God is never absent, never giving up on his people, always moving history forward toward the perfection of his love for humanity, the redemption of all things.

IT CHANGED THE WAY I SEE MYSELF. Reading the Bible as the story of God's redemptive mission has turned me inside out by bringing God's love for the world into every dimension of my faith and life. I used to read the Bible so that I could be right. Now I read it so that I can be redemptive. Don't get me wrong. We can't be redemptive if we're not right about the gospel. But we have no reason to be right if we're not redemptive. It also helps me remember that what God has done in my life—saving me, forgiving me, remaking me, gifting me, guiding me, protecting me, and blessing me—is not just for my sake but also for the sake of the world. Reading the Bible as the story of God's mission provides a rationale for my calling as an educator, a deep conviction that what I do in the classroom has to matter in the world, in the lives of those who do not yet know Christ.

IT CHANGED THE WAY I SEE THE WORLD. I used to read the Bible defensively with an "us versus them" mentality. That approach made me angry and judgmental toward people who didn't believe the way I did and didn't live the way I thought they ought to live. Reading the Bible as the story of God's redemptive mission, however, stirs my heart to compassion and creates a deep longing for those who do not know the Redeemer. I weep for the lost and grieve for those who do not know the One who can make them whole.

To be honest, it's hard to think of anything in my life that hasn't been changed through reading the Bible as the story of God's redemptive mission.

I've returned many, many times to the conversation with the man on that flight out of Paris. If I could rewind my life and have another chance to answer "What is that book about?" I would say to him, "It's a redemption story, a magnificent tale of God's love. It points us to the cross where Jesus died to rescue us from our sin and restore us to the life he created us to have. Reading it has changed my life. And it can change yours too."

And it will change yours too.

NOTES

PART 1. STORY

1. Jonathan Haidt, *The Righteous Mind: Why Good People Are Divided by Politics and Religion* (New York: Vintage Books, 2013), 328.
2. Jonathan Gottschall, *The Storytelling Animal: How Stories Make Us Human* (New York: Mariner Books, 2012), xiv.

CHAPTER 1. THE ONE TRUE STORY

1. Lesslie Newbigin, *The Gospel in a Pluralist Society* (Grand Rapids, MI: Eerdmans, 1989), 15, quoted in Craig B. Bartholomew and Michael W. Goheen, "Story and Biblical Theology" in *Out of Egypt: Biblical Theology and Biblical Interpretation*, ed. Craig Bartholomew, Mary Healy, Karl Möller, and Robin Parry (Grand Rapids, MI: Zondervan, 2004), 150.
2. Jonathan Gottschall, "Why Fiction Is Good for You," *The Boston Globe*, April 29, 2012, https://www.bostonglobe .com/ideas/2012/04/28/why-fiction-good-for-you-how -fiction-changes-your-world/nubDy1P3viDj2PuwGwb3KO /story.html.
3. According to a 2017 Barna study, 13 percent of Americans are hostile skeptics who "view the Bible as a book of teachings written by men and intended to manipulate and control other people." Barna.com, "State of the Bible 2017: Top Findings," April 4, 2017, https://www.barna.com /research/state-bible-2017-top-findings/.

4. The near reference for the end of the set period of time implied in the very first verse of the Bible is the seventh day of the creation story. That is most likely what Moses had in mind as the author of the text. However, the remarkable similarity between the first and last chapters of the Bible (Genesis 1–2 and Revelation 21–22) support the idea that, through the inspiration of the Holy Spirit, the opening words of the Bible, "In the beginning," imply a bigger end to an even bigger story than the seven days of creation.

5. Gottschall, "Why Fiction Is Good for You."

6. Chaturvedi Badrinath, quoted in Bartholomew and Goheen, "Story and Biblical Theology," 151. See also Lesslie Newbigin, *A Walk through the Bible* (Louisville: Westminster John Knox, 1999), 4.

CHAPTER 2. ONE BIG STORY, TWO BIG WORDS

1. Francesca Street, "1 in 50 People Finds Love on an Airplane, Study Claims," CNN Travel, updated August 30, 2018, https://www.cnn.com/travel/article/fall-in-love-airplane/index.html.

2. "Number of Scheduled Passengers Boarded by the Global Airline Industry from 2004 to 2018 (in Millions)," accessed October 25, 2018, Statista.com, https://www.statista.com/statistics/564717/airline-industry-passenger-traffic-globally/#0.

3. "'It Just Felt Right': Woman Adopts Baby after Sitting Next to Pregnant Woman on a Plane," ABC News, April 10, 2018, https://abcnews.go.com/US/felt-woman-adopts-baby-sitting-pregnant-woman-plane/story?id=54378168.

4. Lindsey Ashcraft and Eun Kyung Kim, "Woman Adopts Son of Stranger She Met on a Plane: 'He's Just a Blessing,'" Today.com, April 12, 2018, https://www.today.com/parents/woman-adopts-son-stranger-she-met-plane-he-s-just-t126943.

5. Samantha Snipes, "Stranger on Airplane Adopts Woman's Newborn Son after Chance Encounter: 'I Felt as If We Had Been Friends for Years,'" LoveWhatMatters.com, accessed October 25, 2018, https://www.lovewhatmatters.com /stranger-on-airplane-adopts-womans-newborn-son-after -chance-encounter-i-felt-as-if-we-had-been-friends-for-years/.

6. "It Just Felt Right."

7. Ashcraft and Kim, "Woman Adopts Son of Stranger."

8. Char Adams, "Stranger on Plane Adopts Woman's Son after Chance Encounter: 'They Were Meant for Each Other,'" People.com, April 11, 2018, https://people.com/human -interest/samantha-snipes-plane-son-adopt-chance/.

9. For an excellent and exhaustive exposition of the mission of God as a hermeneutical paradigm, see Christopher J. H. Wright, *The Mission of God: Unlocking the Bible's Grand Narrative* (Downers Grove, IL: InterVarsity Press, 2006).

10. Mark S. Young and Priscilla R. Young, "Marriage and the Mission of God" in *Marriage: Its Foundation, Theology, and Mission in a Changing World*, ed. Curt Hamner, John Trent, Rebekah J. Byrd et al. (Chicago: Moody Publishers, 2018), 356.

11. Wright, *Mission of God*, 29.

12. Wright, *Mission of God*, 103.

13. David Filbeck, *Yes, God of the Gentiles Too: The Missionary Message of the Old Testament* (Wheaton, IL: Billy Graham Center, 1994), 10.

14. Filbeck, *Yes, God of the Gentiles Too*, 10.

CHAPTER 3. CREATION

1. There are several different approaches to integrating science and the Bible. They tend to fall into three different groups: creation science, intelligent design, and theistic evolution. Each approach offers much to consider. For

a good place to see how we came to think that the Bible and science are at war with one another, see the article by Timothy Larsen, "'War Is Over, If You Want It': Beyond the Conflict between Faith and Science," *Perspectives on Science and Faith* 60, no. 3 (September 2008): 148–50.

2. Translation of *Rig-Veda* text provided by Wendy Doniger O'Flaherty, trans., *The Rig Veda: An Anthology: One Hundred and Eight Hymns*, Penguin Classics (Harmondsworth, Middlesex: Penguin Books, 1986), 25–26.

3. These and other creation stories and translations of ancient texts are found in Ellen van Wolde, *Stories of the Beginning: Genesis 1–11 and Other Creation Stories* (Ridgefield, CT: Morehouse Publishing, 1997). For a helpful review and critique of van Wolde's thinking, see https://reasons.org/explore/publications/tnrtb/read/tnrtb/2010/04/23/did-god-create-heaven-and-earth-or-just-separate-them-an-analysis-of-ellen-van-wolde's-hypothesis-part-1-(of-2).

4. See also 1 Corinthians 8:6.

5. David Foster Wallace, "Transcription of the 2005 Kenyon Commencement Address—May 21, 2005," accessed December 15, 2018, https://web.ics.purdue.edu/~drkelly/DFWKenyonAddress2005.pdf.

6. J. Richard Middleton concludes, "When the clues within the Genesis text are taken together with comparative studies of the ancient Near East, they lead to what we could call a functional—or even missional—interpretation of the image of God in Genesis 1:26–27 (in contradistinction to substantialistic or relational interpretations). On this reading, the *imago Dei* designates the royal office or calling of human beings as God's representatives and agents in the world, granted authorized power to share in God's rule or administration of the earth's resources and creatures." J. Richard Middleton, *The Liberating Image:*

The Imago Dei *of Genesis 1* (Grand Rapids, MI: Brazos, 2005), 27.

7. Eugene H. Merrill, *Everlasting Dominion: A Theology of the Old Testament* (Nashville: B&H Group, 2006), 136.

8. Mike Mason, *The Mystery of Marriage: 20th Anniversary Edition* (Colorado Springs: Multnomah Books, 1985, 2005), 50.

9. For a song that expresses the idea that we are made to worship God, see the lyrics of "Made to Worship," written by Chris Tomlin, Ed Cash, and Stephan Sharp, from the album *See the Morning* (sixsteps Records/Sparrow Records, 2006).

10. Victor P. Hamilton, *The Book of Genesis 1–17*, New International Commentary on the Old Testament (Grand Rapids, MI: Eerdmans, 1990), 159.

11. NET Bible translator's note on "lamp" in Proverbs 20:27.

12. See G. K. Beale, *The Temple and the Church's Mission: A Biblical Theology of the Dwelling Place of God*, New Studies in Biblical Theology 17 (Downers Grove, IL: InterVarsity Press, 2004); and Allen P. Ross, *Recalling the Hope of Glory: Biblical Worship from the Garden to the New Creation* (Grand Rapids, MI: Kregel, 2006).

13. See Carolyn Custis James, *Lost Women of the Bible: The Women We Thought We Knew* (2005; repr., Grand Rapids, MI: Zondervan, 2008), 37–38.

CHAPTER 4. FALL

1. Leonid Taycher, "Books of the World, Stand Up and Be Counted! All 129,864,880 of You," Booksearch.blogspot.com, August 5, 2010, http://booksearch.blogspot.com/2010/08/books-of-world-stand-up-and-be-counted.html.

2. Statistia.com, "Leading Online Print Book Genres in the United States in 2017, by Revenue (in Million U.S. Dollars)," accessed September 22, 2018, https://www.statista.com/statistics/322187/book-genres-revenue/.

3. Barbara Hoffert, "What's Hot Now? Materials Survey 2018," LibraryJournal.com, February 6, 2018, https://www .libraryjournal.com/?detailStory=whats-hot-now-materials -survey-2018.

4. For more on the Hebrew wordplay between the words translated "crafty" (*arum*) in Genesis 3:1 and "naked" (*arom*) in Genesis 2:25, see the NET Bible notes on Genesis 3:1.

5. For example, see Proverbs 12:23 and 13:16.

6. Old Testament scholar Tremper Longman III describes this reality well: "Adam and Eve's sin, to use Paul's language, introduced sin into the world. Their sin so corrupted the divine-human, human-human, and creation-human relationships that we are born into a warped and distorted world. It is not possible for us not to sin. . . ." Tremper Longman III, *Genesis*, Story of God Bible Commentary (Grand Rapids, MI: Zondervan, 2016), 72.

7. Rebellion against the gods is a common theme in the stories of ancient cultures. For instance, the ancient Babylonians and Egyptians both had myths that included human rebellion against their gods. These stories reflect the universal human experience of evil. The biblical account, however, departs dramatically from other ancient Near Eastern mythologies about human rebellion in the way God responds to it.

8. I heard Briscoe say this at a conference I attended in the late 1980s. It may also be accessed by searching for his two-part message entitled "Finding Spiritual Wisdom," broadcast from the *Telling the Truth* radio program hosted at https://www.oneplace.com/.

9. If the Hebrew verb (*halak*) is understood to mean "walking" in Genesis 3:8, the passage describes a theophany, which is to say that God is appearing in some kind of

physical presence. But this phenomenon occurs nowhere else in Genesis 1–3.

10. The term "storm" or "whirlwind" (Hebrew *se'arah*) is used in Job 38:1 to describe how the Lord spoke to Job. In Psalm 29 we see the power of the sound of God's voice (Hebrew *qol*).

11. Old Testament scholar John Walton points out that the Hebrew word translated "day" (*yom*) can also mean "storm" in Akkadian where it is used to refer to a god coming in judgment. He proposes that Genesis 3:8 could possibly be translated "They heard the roar of the LORD moving about in the garden in the wind of the storm." Walton adds that this translation is "a possibility, but one that can only be held tentatively." John H. Walton, *Genesis*, NIV Application Commentary (Grand Rapids, MI: Zondervan, 2001), 224.

12. The Hebrew text uses similar terms to describe the pain of childbirth and the painful toil of working the earth. The words refer to physical pain and emotional distress.

13. World Health Organization, "Maternal and Reproductive Health," Global Health Observatory (GHO) Data, accessed October 28, 2019, https://www.who.int/gho/maternal_health/en/.

14. Just as we should not assume that childbirth would have been painless before the fall, so we should not assume that causing the earth to bring forth its goodness would have happened without hard work. What has changed is that both the pain of childbirth and the pain of work could end up in nothing more than futility.

15. Walton, *Genesis*, 231.

16. The Hebrew word translated "Eve" (*chawwah*) is phonetically similar to the Hebrew verb "to live" (*chayah*).

CHAPTER 5. REDEMPTION IN THE OLD TESTAMENT

1. The Lord changes Abram's name to Abraham in Genesis 17:5. I am using "Abraham" throughout the book because it is the name most Bible readers know and the name used for Abram in the New Testament.

2. Whereas "all people" might imply every single individual, we use the plural form "all peoples" to refer to all ethno-linguistic groups of people.

3. W. Ross Blackburn, *The God Who Makes Himself Known: The Missionary Heart of the Book of Exodus*, New Studies in Biblical Theology (Downers Grove, IL: InterVarsity Press, 2012), 212.

4. Blackburn, *The God Who Makes Himself Known*, 50.

5. See Claude Monet, *The Japanese Footbridge*, 1899, oil on canvas, 32 × 40" (81.3 × 101.6 cm), National Gallery of Art, Washington, DC, https://www.nga.gov/collection/art-object-page.74796.html.

CHAPTER 6. REDEMPTION IN THE NEW TESTAMENT

1. The Latin phrase that Luther used is *Crux probat omnia.* See Martin Luther, *Luthers Werke: Kritische Gesamtausgabe* [*Schriften*], 73 vols. (Weimar: Hermann Böhlau, 1883–2009), vol. 5, pt. 179, p. 31.

2. Fleming Rutledge, *The Crucifixion: Understanding the Death of Jesus Christ* (Grand Rapids, MI: Eerdmans, 2015), 44; emphasis original.

3. There are two primary Hebrew verbs used for "ransom" in the Old Testament. The first verb is *padah*, which means "ransom" or "redeem," and this term refers to substituting a required person or an animal for something that belongs to God. According to the Law, the firstborn of the livestock and the firstborn child belong to God. You could redeem the firstborn animal and firstborn child by paying a price.

See Exodus 13:1–16. The second verb is *ga'al*, which means "redeem" or "act as a kinsman-redeemer." This is a legal term for delivering or recovering someone as property through a family relation. For instance, if someone in your family is enslaved or brought into servitude because they became indebted, a kinsman-redeemer (*go'el*) can come and pay for the family member's release from servitude. Similar to the idea of *padah*, *ga'al* denotes the act of paying a price for bringing someone back into a former relationship or restoring their former status. A person who buys the right to bring someone back into relationship is called a "redeemer." Probably the most well-known example of a kinsman-redeemer in the Old Testament is the story of Boaz redeeming the widow Ruth from another relative who had familial rights to redeem her dead husband's land and take her as a wife. Boaz pays that other relative the redemption price so he can bring Ruth into his family.

4. This same language is very powerfully used in the apostle John's vision in Revelation 5:1–10. In the heavenly throne room, there is a scroll that must be unrolled, an illustration for the unfolding of human history. An angel asks, "Who is worthy to break the seals and open the scroll?" (v. 2), meaning who is worthy to bring to pass God's plan for the end of human history? They look but no one can be found. Finally, they see the Lamb who was slain, and he is deemed to be worthy to open the scroll (vv. 3–5). In verses 9–10, we read that all in the heavenly throne room sang a new song of worship to the Lamb: "You are worthy to take the scroll and to open its seals, because you were slain, and with your blood you *purchased* for God persons from every tribe and language and people and nation. You have made them to be a kingdom and priests to serve our God, and they will reign on the earth" (emphasis

added). What does the Messiah accomplish through this payment of ransom with his own blood? Humanity has been rescued from the penalty of sin and can now be restored to life in fellowship with God.

5. It's no wonder that both Jesus (Matthew 24:4–8; John 16:19–24) and the apostle Paul (1 Thessalonians 5:2–3) use the language of childbirth to describe the consummation of redemption in the second coming of Christ.

6. See Søren Agersnap, *Baptism and the New Life: A Study of Romans 6:1–14* (Aarhus, Denmark: Aarhus University Press, 1999), 401, cited in Craig Blomberg, *A New Testament Theology* (Waco, TX: Baylor University Press), 695.

7. C. S. Lewis, *The Last Battle* (New York: Collier Books, 1956), 171.

PART 3. CHARACTERS

1. "5 Important Characters to Have in Every Story," NY Book Editors blog, accessed April 5, 2020, https://nybookeditors .com/2018/01/5-important-characters-to-have-in -every-story/.

CHAPTER 7. CHOSEN

1. Out of the almost 38 million people living in Poland at that time, there were only five thousand members of Baptist churches.

2. Although it's rare in the New Testament to find someone called to a specific task or region, one example is Acts 16:9–10, where Paul sees a vision of a man begging for help and concludes that he is "called" to go and preach the gospel to those in Macedonia.

3. As we noted earlier in Genesis 17:5, God renames Abram, "Abraham," to indicate that he will be a father of many nations.

4. There were dozens of gods, demigods, and named spirits in ancient Mesopotamia. Many were associated with the sun, moon, and stars. See Jeremy Black and Anthony Green, *Gods, Demons and Symbols of Ancient Mesopotamia: An Illustrated Dictionary* (London: British Museum Press, 1992).

5. Many evangelical Bible scholars would see the book of Job as a pre-Abrahamic story, even though it's situated well after Genesis in the canon of the Old Testament.

6. As we have noted, Abraham was a descendant of Shem. Genesis 9:26–27 tells us that Noah blessed Shem above his brothers, Ham and Japheth, apparently because he had honored his father despite Noah's shameful behavior described in Genesis 9:20–21. God's choice of Abraham is in line with this blessing, but it doesn't serve as a rationale for that choice.

7. I am indebted to Christopher J. H. Wright for this translation. See Wright, *Mission of God*, 200.

8. Old Testament scholar William Dumbrell describes God's command to Abraham as follows: "In short, the call was to abandon all natural connections, to surrender all social customs and traditions, to leave land, clan and family. These were the very areas of strong attachment which in the ancient world would have been thought to provide ultimate personal security. Whatever binds him to the past is to be discarded in this call which now comes to him to be the father of a new nation." W. J. Dumbrell, *Covenant and Creation: A Theology of Old Testament Covenants* (1984; repr., Eugene, OR: Wipf and Stock, 2009), 57.

9. Refrain from "Trust and Obey," lyrics by John H. Sammis (1887). One of the last verses of this hymn reads, "But we never can prove / The delights of his love / Until all on the altar we lay; / For the favor he shows, / And the joy he bestows, / Are for them who will trust and obey."

10. The Hebrew word for "covenant" (*berith*) means "a solemn commitment guaranteeing promises or obligations undertaken by one or both covenanting parties." P. R. Williamson, "Covenant" in *Dictionary of the Old Testament: Pentateuch*, ed. T. Desmond Alexander and David W. Baker, IVP Bible Dictionary Series 1 (Downers Grove, IL: InterVarsity Press, 2003), 139.

11. Many scholars believe that when Abraham is called a "Hebrew" in Genesis 14:13, that name implies an identity as someone without a permanent residence.

12. It is interesting to note that Abraham is revered in all three of the world's largest monotheistic religions: Judaism, Christianity, and Islam.

13. See Wright, *Mission of God*, 201n18.

14. The ESV translation of 12:2, "so that you will be a blessing," captures the meaning of the structure well.

15. It is important to see that God's purpose of establishing a people is not just to be able to curse everyone else. The line "and whoever curses you I will curse" differs grammatically and syntactically from the promise to bless those who bless Abram. Old Testament scholar Patrick Miller translates this line almost as an aside to the promises to bless: "and should there be one who regards you with contempt I will curse him." Patrick D. Miller, "Syntax and Theology in Genesis 12.3a," in *Israelite Religion and Biblical Theology: Collected Essays*, Journal for the Study of the Old Testament Supplement Series 267 (Sheffield, UK: Sheffield Academic Press, 2000), 495.

16. N. T. Wright, *After You Believe: Why Christian Character Matters* (New York: HarperOne, 2010), 104.

17. For example, God's plan to bless all peoples through his chosen people is repeated to Abraham in Genesis 18:18 and 22:17–18, to Isaac in 26:3–4, and to Jacob in 28:13–14.

18. See the ESV translation of Galatians 3:8.

19. Jesus also confirms the certainty that this promise will be
    fulfilled. In Matthew 8:10–11, after witnessing the faith of
    a Gentile, Jesus says, "Truly I tell you, I have not found any-
    one in Israel with such great faith. I say to you that many
    will come from the east and the west, and will take their
    places at the feast with Abraham, Isaac and Jacob in the
    kingdom of heaven." Jesus affirms that Gentiles also ("all
    peoples") will enjoy the feast of blessing with the patriarchs
    when they come to know and worship Abraham's God.

20. God has chosen us to be his people. But what does that
    mean? Unfortunately, there is a lot of confusion around
    this question. Controversies about terms such as *election* and
    predestination create more heat than they shed light on the
    question of what it means to be God's chosen people. One
    problem is that we tend to read the Bible as individualists
    and assume that God chooses some individuals for salva-
    tion but not others. This reading of the Bible comes from a
    perspective that none of the biblical authors likely shared.
    Instead, biblical authors thought in communal or collec-
    tivistic terms; in other words, their first thought was for the
    group as a whole. In the Bible, God's choosing of Abraham
    is representative of him choosing an entire nation of those
    who follow him. And God's choosing is never intended to
    be a source of arrogance or superiority in relation to others.
    Rather, we are chosen to service not to privilege. With God,
    the goal of choosing (electing) one people is the blessing
    of all peoples. The constant temptation of God's people
    throughout the history of the church "has been to forget the
    missional purpose of election and to stress only privilege,
    salvation, and the status of being a recipient." Michael W.
    Goheen, *A Light to the Nations: The Missional Church and the
    Biblical Story* (Grand Rapids, MI: Baker Academic, 2011), 31.

CHAPTER 8. UNIQUE

1. Note the change in my translation of Exodus 19:5. Most English translations read "*Although* the whole earth is mine," but I prefer "*Because* the whole earth is mine" (emphases added). The language and syntax of the phrase support either translation. "Because the whole earth is mine" gives a sense of purpose or rationale to what follows.

2. John Durham contends that Israel was to be "committed to the extension throughout the world of the ministry of Yahweh's Presence . . . a kingdom run not by politicians depending upon strength and connivance but by priests depending on faith in Yahweh, a servant nation instead of a ruling nation." See John I. Durham, *Exodus*, Word Biblical Commentary 3 (Waco, TX: Word Books, 1987), 263. See also Merrill, *Everlasting Dominion*, 160–61.

3. For two examples of the many verses where God's uniqueness is described, see Exodus 8:10 and Jeremiah 10:6.

4. See Christopher J. H. Wright, *Old Testament Ethics for the People of God* (Downers Grove, IL: IVP Academic, 2004).

5. I am indebted to John Durham for the concept of God's people as a "showcase" (see his *Exodus* commentary cited above).

6. Although the NIV and ESV translate the Greek conjunction (*hopōs*) at the beginning of this clause as "that," the word indicates purpose or result in most of its occurrences in the New Testament.

7. Karen H. Jobes, *1 Peter*, Baker Exegetical Commentary on the New Testament (Grand Rapids, MI: Baker Academic, 2005), 163.

CHAPTER 9. SHAPED

1. Michael Frost, "ReThinking Witness" (Session 5, Exponential East 2014 Conference, Orlando, FL, April 30, 2014),

https://exponential.org/resource-videos/michael-frost
-rethinking-witness-from-2014-east/. See also Michael
Frost, *Surprise the World! The Five Habits of Highly Missional
People* (Colorado Springs: NavPress, 2016).

2. First Peter 3:15 says, "But in your hearts revere Christ as
Lord. Always be prepared to give an answer to everyone
who asks you to give the reason for the hope that you have.
But do this with gentleness and respect." Peter assumes
that our lives will be so shaped by the hope of the gospel
that people will ask us to explain why we live the way we do.

3. Goheen, *A Light to the Nations*, 52–53. The full quote reads,
"Israel's life shaped by God's torah is to stand in contrast to
the nations, a light shining in the midst of pagan darkness.
Sadly, Israel's history too often shows its failure to be God's
light: in succumbing to other religious spirits, it becomes
part of the darkness that it had been sent to dispel."

4. "Global Trends: Forced Displacement in 2018," United
Nations High Commissioner for Refugees (UNHCR),
accessed March 2, 2020, unhcr.org/globaltrends2018/.

5. Leviticus 18 vividly describes the perverse lifestyles practiced
by the inhabitants of the land.

6. Gerhard Lohfink, *Does God Need the Church? Toward a
Theology of the People of God*, trans. Linda M. Maloney
(Collegeville, MN: Liturgical Press, 1999), 27. Lohfink is
a New Testament scholar who since 1986 has lived and
worked as a theologian for the Catholic Integrated Community. The full quote reads, "God begins in a small way,
at one single place in the world. There must be a place,
visible, tangible, where the salvation of the world can begin: that is, where the world becomes what it is supposed
to be according to God's plan. Beginning at that place,
the new thing can spread abroad, but not through persua-
sion, not through indoctrination, not through violence.

Everyone must have the opportunity to come and see. All must have the chance to behold and test this new thing."

7. "Mrs. Meir Says Moses Made Israel Oil-Poor," *New York Times*, June 11, 1973, https://www.nytimes.com/1973/06/11/archives/mrs-meir-says-moses-made-israel-oilpoor.html.

8. In Exodus 3:8, God describes the land of Israel as "a good and spacious land, a land flowing with milk and honey."

9. James V. Brownson, Inagrace T. Dietterich, Barry A. Harvey, and Charles C. West, *StormFront: The Good News of God*, The Gospel and Our Culture Series (Grand Rapids, MI: Eerdmans, 2003), 17.

10. "The 2017 Imagination Report: What Kids Want to Be When They Group Up," Fatherly, December 22, 2017, https://www.fatherly.com/love-money/work-money/the-2017-imagination-report-what-kids-want-to-be-when-they-grow-up/.

11. For the first few instances of this phrase in the Old Testament, see Deuteronomy 12:8; Judges 17:6; and 21:25.

12. The books of 1 and 2 Samuel, 1 and 2 Kings, and 1 and 2 Chronicles provide the historical narrative for all of the prophetic books.

13. See 2 Samuel 7:18–19. Although the translation of this passage is difficult, the ESV captures the significance of this event well: "Then King David went in and sat before the LORD and said, 'Who am I, O Lord GOD, and what is my house, that you have brought me thus far? And yet this was a small thing in your eyes, O Lord GOD. You have spoken also of your servant's house for a great while to come, *and this is instruction for mankind*, O Lord GOD!'" (emphasis added). The italicized phrase indicates that the establishment of an eternal kingdom is a reality that all humanity must know and respond to.

14. Many scholars believe that the Queen of Sheba likely came

from the southern region of the Arabian peninsula, where modern-day Yemen can be found.

CHAPTER 10. SENT

1. John 20:4 contains one of the most human elements of the Bible. For some reason, John believes it is important to note that he got to the tomb ahead of Peter after they both went running to see if Mary's report was true. Makes me smile every time I read it.

2. Most commentators assume that Jesus spoke a blessing of *shalom* over them. See D. A. Carson, *The Gospel According to John*, Pillar New Testament Commentary (Leicester, UK: Inter-Varsity Press; Grand Rapids, MI: Eerdmans, 1991), 647.

3. See Matt Jenson, *The Gravity of Sin: Augustine, Luther, and Barth on 'homo incurvatus in se'* (London: T&T Clark, 2006).

4. Although "go" is not grammatically an imperative, it essentially functions as a command in the sentence. Grant Osborne comments on this verse, "The circumstantial participle 'go'... followed by the main verb is a common Matthean stylistic trait, and it becomes in effect another imperative.... 'Go' is the operative act, as now God's people are no longer to stay in Jerusalem and be a kind of 'show 'n' tell' for the nations but they are actively to go and take the message to the nations." Grant R. Osborne, *Matthew: Zondervan Exegetical Commentary on the New Testament* (Grand Rapids, MI: Zondervan, 2010), 1080.

5. Goheen writes, "Jesus does not send here eleven discrete individuals . . . each with his own responsibility to bear witness to the gospel; this way of reading the mission mandate in light of the Western missionary experience has led us astray. This is not a *task* assigned to isolated *individuals*; it is an *identity* given to a *community*. . . . [Lesslie]

Newbigin notes that Jesus' commission to this community 'is the launching *of the church*. It is a movement launched in the public life of the world. It has no life except in this sending.... The church ... [is] a body thrust out into the world to draw all people to Christ. The church's being is in that sending.'" Goheen, *A Light to the Nations*, 115–16, citing Lesslie Newbigin, *Mission in Christ's Way: A Gift, a Command, an Assurance* (Chester Heights, PA: Friendship Press, 1988), 22–23.

6. In Acts 1:3, Luke writes that Jesus "gave many convincing proofs that he was alive." The Greek word translated "convincing proof" (*tekmērion*) is rendered in a number of languages as "'that which causes one to know for sure' or '...with certainty.'" See Johannes P. Louw and Eugene A. Nida, eds., *Greek-English Lexicon of the New Testament Based on Semantic Domains*, 2 vols. (New York: United Bible Societies, 1988), 1:28.45.

7. W. D. Davies and Dale C. Allison Jr., *A Critical and Exegetical Commentary on the Gospel According to Saint Matthew*, vol. 3, *Commentary on Matthew XIX–XXVIII*, International Critical Commentary (Edinburgh: T&T Clark, 1997), 684. Similarly, N. T. Wright writes, "Just as Jesus taught his followers to pray that God's kingdom would come on earth as in heaven, so now he claims that all authority in heaven and on earth has been given to him, and on that basis he commands the disciples to go and make it happen—to work, in other words, as agents of that authority . . . resurrection doesn't mean escaping from the world: it means mission to the world based on Jesus's lordship over the world." N. T. Wright, *Surprised by Hope: Rethinking Heaven, the Resurrection, and the Mission of the Church* (New York: HarperOne, 2008), 235.

8. Jesus had already told his disciples that only the Father

knows when the Messiah will establish the kingdom. See
Matthew 24:36 and Mark 13:32.

CHAPTER 11. EXILED

1. In Matthew 16:13, Jesus asked his disciples the same
   question but of himself: "Who do people say the Son of
   Man is?"
2. Jobes, *1 Peter*, 163.
3. Jobes, *1 Peter*, 170.
4. Scot McKnight, *1 Peter*, NIV Application Commentary
   (Grand Rapids, MI: Zondervan, 1996), 117.
5. Darrell L. Guder, "Missional Church: From Sending to
   Being Sent," in Darrell L. Guder, ed., Lois Barrett,
   Inagrace T. Dietterich, George R. Hunsberger, Alan J.
   Roxburgh, and Craig Van Gelder, *Missional Church: A Vision
   for the Sending of the Church in North America*, The Gospel and
   Our Culture Series (Grand Rapids, MI: Eerdmans, 1998), 6.

Help us get the word out!

Our Daily Bread Publishing exists to feed the soul with the Word of God.

If you appreciated this book, please let others know.

- Pick up another copy to give as a gift.
- Share a link to the book or mention it on social media.
- Write a review on your blog, on a bookseller's website, or at our own site (odb.org/store).
- Recommend this book for your church, book club, or small group.

Connect with us:

 @ourdailybread

 @ourdailybread

 @ourdailybread

Our Daily Bread Publishing
PO Box 3566
Grand Rapids, Michigan 49501 USA

 books@odb.org